The Nourishing Traditions Cookbook for Children

Suzanne Gross and Sally Fallon Morell

Illustrations by Angela Eisenbart

Cover by Kim Waters

THE
NOURISHING TRADITIONS
COOKBOOK FOR CHILDREN

Teaching Children to Cook
the Nourishing Traditions Way

Suzanne Gross
Sally Fallon Morell

Illustrations by Angela Eisenbart
Cover Design by Kim Waters

A Note to the Reader: The ideas and suggestions contained in this book are for educational purposes only and are not intended as a substitute for appropriate care of a licensed health care practitioner.

Published by:
NewTrends Publishing, Inc.
Brandywine, Maryland 20613

US and Canada Orders (877) 707-1776
www.newtrendspublishing.com   customerservice@newtrendspublishing.com

Available to the trade through
National Book Network 800-462-6420

10,000, 10,000, 5,000, 10,000

ISBN
0-9823383-3-3   978-0-9823383-3-9
PRINTED IN THE UNITED STATES OF AMERICA

Contents

Introduction
(for parents and teachers)

Cooking with children can be challenging. Most kitchens are not designed with children in mind. The counters and cupboards are usually too high for them to reach. Giving children a stool to stand on solves this problem but also makes it easier for them to reach potentially dangerous items, like sharp knives, hot stoves and electrical appliances.

Cooking with children can also be messy. Spills, wasted food and broken dishes are to be expected, but as the saying goes, don't cry over spilled milk. All the extra effort that goes into cooking with children is worth it.

For one thing, children are more likely to eat food they've helped prepare. Picky eaters will take pride in eating a meal they've cooked themselves, especially if you eat it too and comment on how delicious it is. Cooking with children also provides an opportunity to teach them which foods are healthy and why. It can spark questions about where our food comes from and how it is made.

Unfortunately, most children's cookbooks miss out on this opportunity and instead use not-so-healthy recipes, like recipes for cookies and cupcakes, to make cooking more fun. Even cookbooks that claim to have healthy recipes often call for processed ingredients that come in cans and packages, instead of fresh, whole foods, probably because this makes the recipes easier and quicker to prepare and safer because knives aren't needed. The food is often "cooked" in a microwave, rather than in an oven or on the stove, probably also out of a concern for safety and convenience.

But is this what we want our children to be learning in the kitchen? Do we want them to think it's okay to sacrifice the quality of food for the sake of safety or convenience? And do we really need to tempt children with sweet desserts to get them interested in cooking? Most children enjoy the process of cooking – measuring ingredients, mixing, using kitchen tools – regardless of whether the end result is pudding or pâté.

Turn your kitchen into a classroom (or your classroom into a kitchen)! The measurements involved in cooking can be used to teach numbers, counting, math and fractions, especially when doubling or halving recipes. Reading recipes provides practice in phonics and comprehension. Cooking together, especially if you have more than one child, helps children learn to work co-operatively in a group. When shopping for food, keep your children occupied by asking them to help you find items on your list. Read the labels on packaged foods with your children and discuss why that food is or isn't healthy. Guide your children in how to select the freshest, ripest and highest quality produce. Older children can even be given the responsibility of handling the money and keeping the shopping trip within a budget. Cooking can lead to many other activities and projects, like growing a vegetable garden, raising backyard chickens or composting.

Knowing how to cook is just as valuable (in life) as knowing how to read or write. Food is one of our basic needs. And the quality of our food has a profound impact on our health and ultimately, the quality of our life. If we don't teach our children how to cook nourishing foods, who will? Cooking is rarely taught in schools. Even when it is, the same compromises found in most children's cookbooks are often made out of a concern for safety and convenience.

Many parents feel they don't have time to cook, let alone time to teach their children to cook. And with so many processed foods available, they may not see a reason to. Why cook, when you can buy dinner in a package and have it on the table in a few minutes? After all, there are more important things to do, right?

The perceived convenience of processed foods is an illusion, however, because the more we become dependent on these foods for our sustenance, the more we become plagued with health problems. Allergies, asthma, eczema, recurring infections, tooth decay, diabetes,

ADHD and autism have become so common, that we might even call it "normal" for children to have at least one of these problems. Some children can't even attend school without medication, or they require special education because of their health problems. As any parent of a child with one of these conditions will tell you, there is nothing convenient about this at all. Time saved not having to "slave over a hot stove" is easily outweighed by time spent at doctor visits and sleepless nights caring for a sick child – not to mention the financial stress of medical bills.

We've attempted to keep the content of this book as simple as possible for children to understand, but we expect that parents, teachers and older children may want to know more. The original edition of this book, *Nourishing Traditions* by Sally Fallon and Mary Enig, PhD, is a great resource, as is *Nutrition and Physical Degeneration* by Weston A. Price, DDS. The Weston A. Price Foundation's web site (westonaprice.org) is another excellent resource for further research.

Cooking nourishing foods does take a significant amount of time and effort, even more so when you choose to include your children in the process. If you're a working or single parent, it may not always be possible for you to prepare home-cooked meals, but better some than none. The more we make cooking a priority in our lives, the more we will be able to enjoy our lives in good health.

If you find yourself feeling overwhelmed or discouraged, look at your children's faces. Do you see bright eyes and glowing cheeks? This will assure you that the extra time and effort you put into preparing nourishing food for them is worth it. Or you may see something different, the face of a sick or suffering child who desperately needs nourishing food. Either way, your children will give you the motivation and encouragement you need. And eventually they will become great helpers in the kitchen!

The joy of having radiantly healthy children who eat nourishing food – and even know how to cook it themselves – makes our every effort and sacrifice completely worth it!

Tips for Cooking with Children

Get Organized
Re-organize your kitchen with your children in mind. Put frequently used child-friendly items, like measuring cups, mixing bowls, spoons, spatulas and whisks, within easy reach. Put knives, electrical appliances and other potentially dangerous items out of reach, at least until your children have learned to use these items safely. Children who aren't tall enough to work at the counter comfortably should have a stool or sturdy chair to stand on. If you have space, put a low table in the kitchen for your children to work at.

Follow a Routine
Before cooking, everyone should wash hands and put on an apron. Next, read through the recipe and ask your children to help gather the ingredients and tools needed. Finally, delegate who will do each task. Older children can be given more advanced tasks (such as chopping vegetables or cooking on the stove), while younger children can be given easier tasks (such as measuring, pouring and mixing). Some tasks may require the help of an adult (pulling a hot pan out of an oven, for example). Make sure everyone helps to clean up at the end. Singing or listening to music during clean-up time can encourage cooperation.

Even a Baby Can Do It
To include a baby, sit the baby in a highchair where he or she can observe the kitchen activity. Your baby can also be worn on your back in a carrier. Whenever possible, let your baby touch and taste different foods and play with pots, spoons and other baby-friendly kitchen items.

Plan It with Pictures

To involve your children in creating a weekly meal plan, first, gather pictures of all your family's favorite recipes and possibly some new ones to try. Search for photos or illustrations on the Internet, in cookbooks (like this one) or cooking magazines. Or, your children may want to photograph or draw the pictures themselves. Glue the pictures onto index cards and label them with the name of the recipe. To make the meal plan, select the recipes you and your children would like, then arrange the pictures onto a white board with magnets in a grid pattern, using markers to label the days of the week and the meals (breakfast, lunch and dinner). Or attach the pictures to a series of clotheslines, one for each day of the week or each meal, using paperclips or clothespins. Hang your completed meal plan on the wall in your kitchen.

Kitchen Tools

Each recipe in this book will tell you which tools are needed for that recipe, but here are some of the most commonly used tools, with tips on how to use them and which kinds are best.

Knives

A good way to learn how to use a knife is to practice cutting soft foods, like a banana, with a butter knife. Once you have mastered this, you can start using a serrated knife. Serrated knives are best because they have a jagged edge that is less likely to slip. They're especially good for cutting up foods with smooth skins, like tomatoes. Serrated knives also don't need sharpening like other knives do. Always ask an adult for permission before using a knife.

Cutting Board

Cutting boards protect both your knife and your kitchen counter or table from damage when you are cutting up food. Wood cutting boards are better than plastic because they are less likely to harbor bacteria. You should have at least two cutting boards, one for meat and one for other foods.

Food Chopper

A food chopper is a handy tool for chopping food into small pieces. It can be used instead of a knife.

Mixing Bowls

Mixing bowls come in all sizes, but the larger ones are easier to use. They don't tip over as easily and there's more room to mix the food so it won't spill over the side. Glass or ceramic bowls are best. Pyrex mixing bowls come with handy lids that can be used to keep a batter covered when soaking or for storing leftovers. Large glass measuring cups also make great mixing bowls, especially for liquids or batters that need to be poured.

Egg Beater

A beater can be used not only for eggs, but for mixing batters too. You may find it easier to use than a whisk.

Pots and Pans

When cooking on the stove, use pots and pans made out of stainless steel, cast iron, ceramic or enamel. When baking in the oven, use glass, enamel, stoneware or stainless steel pans. Avoid aluminum and Teflon non-stick cookware.

Caring for Cast Iron
Rinse the pan with hot water immediately after cooking. To remove burned-on food, scrub with coarse salt. Never use soap or steel wool to clean the pan. To prevent rust, dry the pan on the stove over low heat. Rub oil on the pan with a paper towel as needed to keep it shiny.

These materials are toxic and can leach into foods that are cooked in them. Aluminum cookie sheets and muffin tins are okay, as long as they are lined with parchment paper or muffin cups, so that the food doesn't touch the aluminum.

Parchment Paper

Also known as baking paper, this is a safe, non-toxic way to line your baking pans and cookie sheets instead of using aluminum foil or non-stick sprays. A reusable silicone baking mat is also a good option.

Storage Containers

It's best to use glass or ceramic containers for storing foods in the refrigerator and pantry. Glass or ceramic should always be used when soaking, culturing or fermenting foods. Avoid using plastic containers or buying food that is sold in plastic. The chemicals in plastic can easily leach

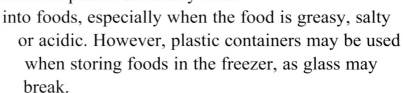

into foods, especially when the food is greasy, salty or acidic. However, plastic containers may be used when storing foods in the freezer, as glass may break.

Food Processor

A food processor makes many tasks in the kitchen easier and faster, whether it's chopping, grating, grinding, whipping or puréeing. A food processor with a powerful motor and a strong blade can be used to grind nuts into nut butter. Food processors can be loud and a bit scary, but they're actually safer to use than a blender, because the motor won't start unless the lid is locked. Remember though, the blade inside is very sharp, so never put your hands inside or touch the blade. Always ask an adult for help when using a food processor.

Handheld Blender
This is a useful tool for making soups and sauces, because you can blend the ingredients right in the pot instead of having to pour them in and out of a blender. This is a tool that should only be used with an adult's help. Be sure to keep the blender submerged while it's running, to prevent spatters.

Grain Mill
A grain mill grinds whole grains into fresh flour. Flour that is freshly ground has more vitamins in it than store-bought flour. It's also higher in enzymes and gives better results when soaking and souring. See Sources (page 223) for recommended grain mills.

Dehydrator
A dehydrator is a special kind of oven that removes moisture from foods without cooking it. When food has no moisture in it, it lasts much longer. Fruits, vegetables and even meat can be saved for a long time without refrigeration by dehydrating them. An oven can also be used to dehydrate food, but a dehydrator is better because

it dries the food at a lower temperature, preserving the enzymes and vitamins in the food. See Sources (page 223) for recommended dehydrators.

Microwave Oven

One tool you won't be needing is a microwave oven. It may seem safer, quicker and easier to use a microwave oven, because it doesn't get hot like an oven or a stove, but studies show that microwaves damage the fats, proteins and vitamins in food, making these nutrients harder for our bodies to digest and even toxic. But there is one good thing a microwave can be used for; it can be used instead as a warm place for soaking grains (see page 145).

Measuring Cups and Spoons

When measuring ingredients for a recipe, you'll need a set of measuring cups and spoons, preferably stainless steel, and a quart-sized glass measuring cup for measuring liquids. More about these tools can be found on the next page.

Apron

Cooking can be messy, so don't forget an apron to keep your clothes clean!

Measuring Guide

Knowing how to measure food is an important skill to have when cooking. It helps you to put the right amount of each ingredient in the recipe. There are several ways to measure food. It can be measured by volume (how big it is) using measuring cups and spoons. It can be measured by weight (how heavy it is) using a scale. Or it can be measured by quantity (how many there are).

Volume (how big it is)

teaspoon

tablespoon
1 tablespoon = 3 teaspoons

cup
1 cup = 16 tablespoons

quart
1 quart = 4 cups

1 stick of butter equals ½ cup or 8 tablespoons

gallon
1 gallon = 4 quarts

Weight (how heavy it is)

pounds/ounces
1 pound = 16 ounces

How much is a pinch?
A pinch is often used to measure salt or spices. It is how much you can pick up with your thumb and forefinger, or about 1/8 teaspoon.

Quantity (how many there are)

3 carrots

1 dozen eggs

How many are in a dozen?
Count the eggs to find out.

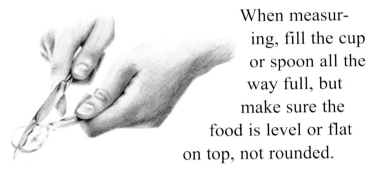

When measuring, fill the cup or spoon all the way full, but make sure the food is level or flat on top, not rounded.

Number of Servings
Most recipes will tell you how many people it serves or how much food it makes. Depending on how many people you are cooking for, a recipe may not make enough or may make too much. You can change a recipe to fit your needs by doubling or tripling it (if you need more) or halving or quartering it (if you need less). This is when it becomes especially helpful to know your measurements, like how many cups are in a quart or how many teaspoons are in a tablespoon. Knowing how to work with fractions is important too, since measurements are often written in fractions, like "½ cup."

The straight edge of a knife can be used to level the food.

When measuring liquids, set the cup on a flat surface at eye-level. If the cup is lower or higher than your eyes, the level of the liquid will look higher or lower than it actually is.

Incredible Eggs!

Incredible Eggs!

Eggs are a very healthy food. Do you know why? Lots of creatures lay eggs. Can you name some? Birds, reptiles and fish all lay eggs. Do you like to eat eggs? Where do your eggs come from?

Do you know what happens to a chicken egg if it is kept safe and warm? A baby chick starts to grow inside! All the nutrients needed to create life are inside an egg. That is why they are so good to eat. When you eat an egg, you are giving your body the fuel it needs to grow and to be strong, healthy and smart.

Some eggs are small, some are big, some are white, some are brown and some even have spots!

Are some eggs better to eat than others? The color and size of an egg tells us what kind of chicken it came from, but it doesn't tell us whether the egg is healthy or not. Healthy eggs come from healthy chickens. What does a chicken need to be healthy? The same things that all creatures (including you) need to be healthy: sunlight, fresh air, exercise and healthy food. Chickens raised inside small cages or factories aren't as healthy as chickens raised on open pastures in the sun eating bugs, worms and greens.

Vegetarian-Fed
This usually means the chickens are fed soy and not allowed to eat bugs and worms, so they cannot be raised on pastures.

Cage-Free, Free-Range
Don't let these terms fool you. Cage-free means the chickens are not in cages, but that doesn't mean they are outside. Free-range means the chickens have access to go outside, but that doesn't mean they actually ever do. In both cases, the chickens may still be raised in a very crowded unhealthy environment.

Did you know that chickens raised in the sun have eggs with bright yellow yolks that look like the sun? The bright color of the yolk means the egg is rich in nutrients and came from a healthy chicken.

Eating healthy starts with knowing where your food comes from. If you buy eggs from a farmer, you can ask the farmer how he raises his chickens. You might even get to visit the farm and see the chickens yourself. Maybe you are lucky enough to have your own chickens. Wherever you get your eggs from, look for ones with bright yolks that come from chickens raised on pastures.

Scrambled Eggs

Serves 2

There are so many ways to eat the incredible egg: fried, scrambled, boiled, in salads, on a sandwich, in soup and even for dessert. Let's get started by learning how to scramble them.

Ready, set...
A good cook reads the entire recipe first before starting. So take a minute to do that now. Do you have all the ingredients and tools needed? Do you understand what needs to be done in each step? If not, ask an adult for help. Most recipes also require measuring spoons and cups, so read the Measuring Guide (page 11) for instructions. All set? Fantastic, it's time to put on your apron and ...**cook**!

1. Crack the eggs into a mixing bowl.
Ask an adult to show you how to do this. Don't be discouraged if you make a mess the first time, this takes a little practice. By the end of this chapter you will be an expert egg cracker!

Ingredients

 2 eggs

pinch sea salt

 2 tablespoons cream

 1 tablespoon butter

Tools

 wooden spoon

wire whisk

fry pan

mixing bowl

2. Add the cream and salt.

3. Beat the eggs with a wire whisk.

4. Melt the butter in a fry pan.

5. Pour the egg mixture into the pan. *Be careful, the pan is very hot!*

6. Stir the egg mixture with a wooden spoon while it is cooking.

7. The eggs are done when they are no longer soupy. Remove them from the pan immediately so they won't burn.

You did it! Yummy, enjoy! Don't forget to help clean up the kitchen when you are finished eating.

Mexican Scrambled Eggs

Serves 4

These scrambled eggs are sure to impress your *familia* or whoever is lucky enough to have you cook this for them.

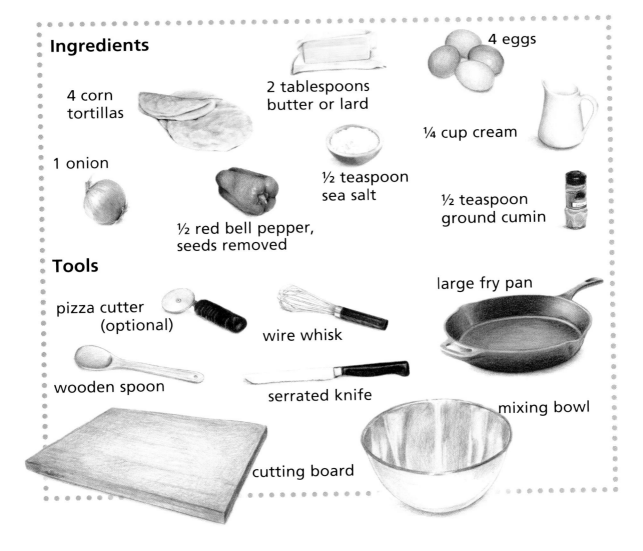

Ingredients

4 corn tortillas

2 tablespoons butter or lard

4 eggs

¼ cup cream

1 onion

½ red bell pepper, seeds removed

½ teaspoon sea salt

½ teaspoon ground cumin

Tools

pizza cutter (optional)

wire whisk

large fry pan

wooden spoon

serrated knife

mixing bowl

cutting board

Know Your Knives
Did you know a sharp knife is safer than a dull one? Knives with a jagged edge are called serrated and are the best knife for you to use, since they are less likely to slip and do not need to be sharpened. Ask an adult to show you how to use a knife correctly and never use a knife unless an adult is with you. Always cut slowly and keep your fingers away from the blade.

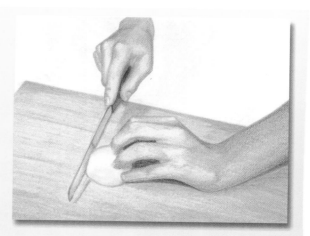

1. Use a pizza cutter or knife to slice the tortillas into thin strips.

2. Melt the butter in a large fry pan over medium heat.

3. Add the tortilla strips and cook until crispy. Stir with a wooden spoon.

4. Chop the onion and bell pepper on a cutting board.

5. Add the onion and bell pepper to the pan and cook until the onion is translucent. *Translucent means your can see through it.*

6. Crack the eggs into a mixing bowl.

7. Add the cream, salt and cumin to the bowl and beat together with a wire whisk.

8. Pour the egg mixture into the pan.

9. Stir the mixture while it is cooking. Cook until the eggs are no longer soupy.

Want to make it even more festive?
Serve with avocado slices, salsa (page 135), sour cream or refried beans (page 158). *Delicioso!* Don't forget to wear your sombrero!

Hard and Soft Boiled Eggs

Hard boiled eggs are great for school lunches, picnics and snacks. Use them to make Deviled Eggs (page 24), Egg Salad (page 192) or Potato Salad (page 194). Or just peel and sprinkle with salt for a quick and easy snack. Soft boiled eggs can be eaten right out of the shell with egg cups and little spoons.

1. Carefully place the eggs in a pot. The pot needs to be big enough so all the eggs can fit side by side with none on top of each other.

2. Fill the pot with cold water until the eggs are covered. *Starting with cold water keeps the eggs from cracking.*

3. Bring the water to a rolling boil over high heat.

4. Turn off the stove, cover the pot with a lid and allow the eggs to cook in the hot water for 10 – 15 minutes (large eggs take longer to cook than medium eggs). For soft boiled eggs, cook only 1 – 2 minutes.

5. Use a slotted spoon to remove the eggs when they are done. Put them in a bowl of ice water to cool.

6. To peel, gently tap the egg until the shell is broken all over. If the shell is difficult to remove, dip the egg in the ice water again.

Ingredients

6 - 12 eggs

Tools

slotted spoon

pot

Deviled Eggs

Serves 6

Deviled eggs are perfect for parties. Serve on a plate of baby lettuce leaves or a deviled egg platter. To make them extra devilish (and nutritious), top with caviar or salmon roe.

Ingredients

¼ cup mayonnaise (page 198)

6 hard boiled eggs, peeled (page 23)

½ teaspoon Dijon mustard

dash sea salt

dash freshly ground pepper

paprika

caviar (optional)

Tools

mixing bowl

serving platter

fork

small spoon

1. Slice the eggs in half lengthwise.

2. To remove the yolks, turn the egg upside down over a mixing bowl and gently bend the egg back until the yolk falls out. Place the whites on a serving platter, hollow side up.

3. Add the mayonnaise, mustard, salt and pepper to the mixing bowl. Mash and stir the mixture with a fork until it's smooth.

4. Using a small spoon, carefully fill the hollow of each egg white with the yolk mixture.

5. Sprinkle paprika on top or top with caviar.

Ruby Eggs
Create hard boiled eggs with stunning ruby-colored whites! Soak peeled eggs in a jar of pickled beet juice (page 132) in the refrigerator for 24 hours.

Egg Eyes (Fried Eggs)

Serves 1

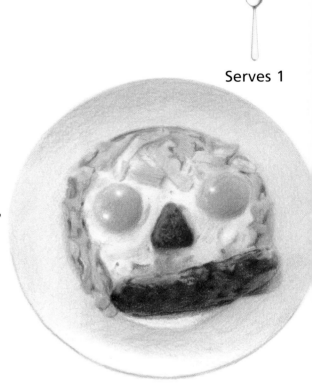

With a bit of creativity you can turn these eggs into a face on your plate. Bacon, sausage or fruits and vegetables can be used to make the nose, mouth and ears. Sauerkraut (page 130) makes great hair!

1. Melt the butter in a fry pan over medium heat.

2. Crack the eggs into the pan, being careful not to break the yolks.

Ingredients

1 tablespoon butter

2 eggs

pinch sea salt

Tools

spatula

fry pan with lid

3. Cover the pan with a lid.

4. Cook until the egg whites are firm and the edges of the yolks are just beginning to turn white.

5. Use a spatula to remove the eggs from the pan.

6. Sprinkle with sea salt.

Egg~Dipped French Toast

Serves 2

French toast is a delicious way to use up old bread. In France, it is called *pain perdu,* which means "lost bread." Although most Americans enjoy French toast for breakfast, in other places of the world it is served for dessert.

Ingredients

2 eggs

2 tablespoons butter

2-4 slices whole grain sourdough bread

2 tablespoons milk

¼ teaspoon ground cinnamon (optional)

Tools

spatula

wire whisk

mixing bowl

fry pan

1. Crack the eggs into a mixing bowl.

2. Add the milk and optional cinnamon and beat together with a wire whisk.

3. Melt the butter in a fry pan over medium heat.

4. Dip the bread, one slice at a time, in the egg mixture until it is covered in egg on both sides. You can cut the bread in half, to make it easier to dip.

5. Carefully transfer the bread to the hot pan. Move the mixing bowl close to the stove so the egg won't drip on the counter or floor. Pour any remaining egg over the top of the bread.

6. Cook the bread until it is lightly browned on the bottom. Then flip it over with a spatula and cook until the other side is also lightly browned.

7. Serve with butter and real maple syrup or fresh strawberries and sweet cheese (page 44).

Greek Omelet

Serves 1

This omelet is made with soft cheese that is added after the omelet is cooked. Serve with olives, cucumber slices, whole wheat pita bread and olive oil and balsamic vinegar for dipping. Tunics and leather sandals are optional.

Ingredients

2 eggs

1 roma tomato

2 tablespoons feta cheese

1 tablespoon butter

dash sea salt

2 tablespoons cream

Tools

wooden spoon

wire whisk

serrated knife

spatula

fry pan

cutting board

mixing bowl

1. Crack the eggs into a mixing bowl. Add the cream and salt. Beat with a wire whisk until the eggs begin to foam.

2. Cut the tomato into tiny pieces.

3. Melt the butter in a fry pan over medium heat.

4. Add the tomato to the pan and stir with wooden spoon to coat the tomato in butter.

5. Pour the eggs over the tomatoes and cover the pan with a lid.

6. Cook for about 5 minutes or until the bottom is golden brown and the top is firm.

7. Remove the pan from the stove. Crumble the feta cheese on top of the omelet. Then fold the omelet in half with a spatula and serve.

Pizza Omelet

Serves 2

Ingredients

4 eggs

1 tablespoon butter

¼ cup cream

tomato paste

mozzarella cheese

Tools

wire whisk

spatula

grater

fry pan

mixing bowl

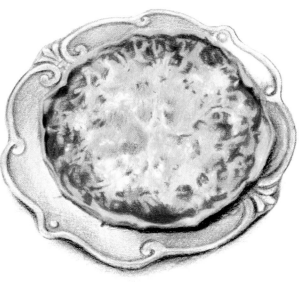

Can you guess what the "crust" for this pizza is made out of?

1. Crack the eggs into a mixing bowl. Add the cream and beat with a wire whisk until the eggs begin to foam.

2. Melt the butter in a fry pan over medium heat.

3. Pour the eggs into the pan and cover with a lid.

4. Cook for about 6 minutes or until the bottom is golden brown and the top is firm.

5. Spread a thin layer of tomato paste on the cooked eggs using a spoon or spatula. Then sprinkle grated cheese on top. Cover with a lid until the cheese melts.

6. Cut the pizza into slices and serve.

Are Raw Eggs Good For You?
Bodybuilders and athletes often eat raw egg yolks. Do you know why? Because raw egg yolks are easier for your body to digest than cooked eggs yolks. That means more of the nutrients in the egg yolk can be used by your body. Egg whites, however, should not be eaten raw. Egg whites are actually harder to digest when raw, and can interfere with your body's ability to absorb biotin, an important vitamin. It's best to eat only the yolks raw and use the whites in recipes that will be cooked.

Can Raw Eggs Make You Sick?
Only one out of every 20,000 eggs is actually contaminated with Salmonella, a bacteria that can make you sick. That means you will probably only come into contact with one or two contaminated eggs during your whole lifetime. Salmonella is almost always found in the white part of the egg, not the yolk, so eating only the yolks raw lowers your chance of getting sick. Plus, if your eggs come from healthy pastured chickens, there's even less of a chance that the eggs will be contaminated. Washing your eggs and avoiding eggs that have any cracks in them is another way to protect yourself.

Egg Yolk Smoothie

Serves 2

This smoothie is made with raw egg yolks, but it really doesn't taste like eggs at all. Use any kind of fruit you like, bananas and strawberries are just a suggestion. Frozen fruit will make a thick and frosty smoothie.

Place all the ingredients in a blender and blend until smooth. Add honey or maple syrup to sweeten, if needed. Pour into glasses and enjoy!

Ingredients

2 egg yolks

¼ cup cream

½ cup raw milk, yogurt or kefir (page 41)

1 banana

6 strawberries

1 tablespoon honey or maple syrup (optional)

Tools

blender

Eggnog

Serves 1

Ingredients

½ cup raw milk

¼ cup cream

pinch nutmeg

1 egg yolk

1 teaspoon maple syrup

Tools

pint-sized glass jar

Eggnog is usually a drink for adults, because it's made with liquor, but this version is non-alcoholic. You can still pretend you're a bartender when making it.

Put all the ingredients in a glass jar. Close the lid tightly and shake until the mixture is frothy. Serve "on the rocks" (in a glass with ice).

How to Separate an Egg

Separating eggs is like a game of ping pong. Crack the egg over a bowl and let some of the egg white fall into the bowl. Pass the yolk back and forth between the eggshell halves until all of the egg white is in the bowl.

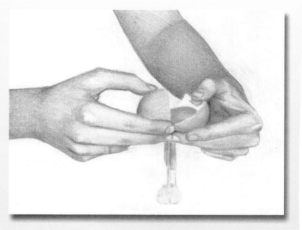

Mighty Milk!

Mighty Milk!

In the previous chapter, we learned that healthy eggs come from healthy chickens. The same is true for milk. Healthy milk comes from healthy cows, sheep and goats.

You've probably heard that milk is a good source of calcium and helps your body build strong bones and teeth. But did you know that your body also needs phosphorus, magnesium and vitamins A, D and K to build strong bones and teeth? Vitamins and minerals work together. If one is missing, the others can't do their job. Enzymes and friendly bacteria also play an important role. They help your body absorb vitamins and minerals from the food you eat.

If you look at a carton of milk, what words do you see? Unless it is raw milk, you will probably see words like *pasteurized, homogenized, low-fat* and *vitamin-D*. Do you know what these words mean? Why is milk pasteurized and homogenized? Why is the fat removed, and why are vitamins added? Actually, milk doesn't need any of these things—if it comes from healthy animals.

Raw milk from healthy animals contains the perfect balance of vitamins, minerals, enzymes and friendly bacteria, which work together to make your body strong. It is nature's perfect food. Nothing needs to be added or taken away.

Unfortunately, most milk comes from dairies where the cows are not very healthy. These dairies operate like factories and treat their cows like machines. The cows are crowded into muddy pens and fed whatever will make them

Pasteurization

When milk is pasteurized, it is heated to a high temperature to kill bacteria in the milk. Most of these bacteria are actually friendly bacteria that help your body digest the milk. This is why many people get a stomach ache or allergies when they drink pasteurized milk. Vitamins B and C and many enzymes that help us absorb vitamins and minerals are also destroyed when milk is pasteurized.

Pasteurized milk is supposed to be safer than raw milk. But pasteurized milk is actually more likely to become contaminated with bad bacteria than raw milk. Raw milk can protect itself from contamination because it is alive with friendly bacteria and special enzymes that kill bad bacteria. Pasteurized milk is a dead food that can easily become contaminated with bad bacteria if it is not stored or handled properly.

Pasteurized milk rots as it gets older and can make you sick if you drink it when it gets too old. Raw milk, on the other hand, never goes bad, it just gets sour. This sour flavor develops because the friendly bacteria in the milk transform the natural sugar (lactose) in the milk into lactic acid. Sour milk is actually easier for your body to digest than fresh milk.

Heat is not as harmful to cream as it is to milk. So it's okay to cook with cream and butter and to use pasteurized cream and butter, but avoid ultra-pasteurized. Ultra-pasteurized milk products are heated to an even higher temperature than pasteurized.

Fake milks
Soy milk, rice milk and other milk substitutes are unhealthy processed foods. They usually contain additives and sweeteners to make them taste better and are enriched with synthetic vitamins. Soy is especially dangerous. Soy disrupts the natural balance of hormones in your body and can prevent your body from absorbing minerals. Beans, grains, nuts and seeds can be healthy for us to eat but they need to be prepared in special ways (see page 142).

produce the most milk for the least amount of money, even if it makes them sick and shortens their lives. Their food is usually a mixture of grain, soy, factory waste (orange peels, almond hulls, cottonseed) and hay. These foods may sound natural, but are they natural for cows to eat?

Cows have a complex digestive system. They have four stomachs. Their stomachs are designed for digesting grass. When other foods are given to cows, it makes them sick because it makes their stomachs too acidic. On most dairies, the sick cows are given antibiotics. The antibiotics make it even harder for the cows'

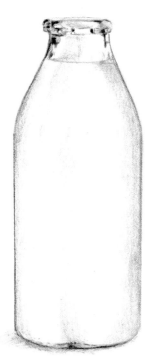

bodies to digest food and they become sicker. In a very short time, the cows become too sick to produce milk anymore and are shipped off to the slaughterhouse. Meat from these sick cows is sold to fast food restaurants and made into hamburgers.

Cows raised on factory farms may produce high quantities of milk for a short time, but this milk is very low in quality. It is missing many important nutrients and is usually not safe to drink raw because the cows aren't healthy.

The only milk that is safe to drink raw is milk that comes from healthy animals. For cows to be healthy, they need to graze on fresh green grass in sunny pastures during the spring, summer and fall. In the winter, they can be fed hay (dried grass), silage (fermented grass and grains) and root vegetables. Cows that are raised this way rarely get sick, but if they do, they should be treated with natural remedies, never antibiotics.

If you need help finding raw grass-fed milk in your area, see page 223.

Homogenization
Cream is lighter than the rest of milk so it naturally rises to the top. Homogenization was invented to prevent the cream from rising to the top. When milk is homogenized, it is forced through microscopic holes that break apart the cream into tiny fat particles. These fat particles can be harmful to our bodies. Milk that is homogenized must also be pasteurized or else enzymes in the milk will turn the fat particles rancid.

Reduced-Fat Milk
Many people think the cream in milk causes heart disease, but cream is actually a very healthy and valuable part of milk. It is the part that contains vitamins A, D, E and K. Your body needs these vitamins to be strong and healthy. When the cream is removed to make low-fat and fat-free milk, these valuable vitamins are lost.

Spiced Milk

Serves 1

Ingredients

1 cup raw milk

1 tablespoon cream

1 teaspoon raw honey

½ teaspoon vanilla

pinch of cinnamon

Tools

pot

mug

spoon

This makes a cozy treat before bedtime or after playing outside on a cold day. The milk in this recipe is gently warmed, not boiled, so the friendly bacteria and enzymes are not harmed. To keep the milk raw, do not heat it higher than 110 degrees. This is just a little warmer than a cow's body temperature of about 101 degrees. A candy thermometer can be used to measure the temperature of the milk. Or a clean finger works too. The milk should feel very warm, but you should be able to keep your finger in it without it burning.

1. Fill a pot with about 2 inches of water. Bring the pot of water to a boil and then turn off the stove.

2. Mix the milk, cream, honey and vanilla together in a mug.

3. Place the mug in the pot of hot water. Stir the milk occasionally until it is warm. This usually takes about 5 minutes.

4. Remove the mug and dry it off with a towel.

5. Sprinkle cinnamon on top.

Kefir

Makes 1½ cups

Kefir is like yogurt but thinner. You can drink it in a glass instead of eating it with a spoon. Both kefir and yogurt are cultured or fermented milk products and are made by adding friendly bacteria to milk. When the milk is kept at a warm temperature, the bacteria grow and turn the milk sour and thick.

If you don't have access to raw milk, kefir made from pasteurized milk is the next best thing. The friendly bacteria in kefir will help your body to digest the pasteurized milk. Use organic, grass-fed, cream-top (unhomogenzied) milk if possible. Avoid ultra-pasteurized milk.

There are many ways to make kefir. This recipe makes a mild kefir that tastes more like yogurt. If you don't like the taste of plain kefir, try it in a fruit smoothie (page 33).

Ingredients

1½ cups raw or pasteurized milk

½ tablespoon kefir grains

Tools

2 pint-sized glass jars

spoon

1. Pour ½ cup milk into a clean pint-sized glass jar and add the kefir grains.

2. Cover the jar with a lid and leave it at room temperature for 12 – 24 hours (12 hours if it is warm in your house, 24 hours if it is cool).

3. Remove the grains with a clean spoon. You can also pour the kefir through a strainer to remove the grains. Put the grains in another clean glass jar with ½ cup milk. Store in the refrigerator until you are ready to make more kefir.

Kefir Grains
The friendly bacteria and yeasts used to make kefir look a bit like cauliflower. These white, rubbery clumps are called kefir grains. You only need a small clump of grains to start making kefir (see page 223 for sources). The grains will grow as you use them. Once they have doubled in size, you can either start making your kefir in larger batches or you can share the extra grains with a friend and show them how to make their own kefir. If you take good care of your kefir grains, you will never need to replace them, as they can be used over and over again.

Benefits of Kefir
The friendly bacteria in kefir are different than the bacteria in yogurt. Kefir bacteria can actually live inside your body and protect you from getting sick. Kefir is very easy to digest, even for those who are lactose-intolerant. Kefir can restore enzymes to your body, which will help you to digest other milk products too. Kefir also contains friendly yeasts that protect your body against harmful yeasts (like Candida albicans).

4. Add 1 cup fresh milk to the kefir you have just made.

5. Cover the jar with a lid and leave it at room temperature for another 12 – 24 hours.

6. Store the finished kefir in the refrigerator.

Cream Cheese

Makes 1 cup

Once you know how to make kefir (page 41), making cream cheese is easy. If you aren't a kefir-maker yet, you can also make cream cheese from store-bought yogurt. Use organic, plain, whole milk yogurt made without additives (the ingredients should include only milk and live active cultures). Yogurt made with milk from grass-fed animals is even better.

1. Set a strainer on top of a bowl. The bowl needs to be big enough to hold 2 cups of liquid below the strainer, without the liquid touching the strainer.

2. Line the inside of the strainer with a thin dish towel.

Ingredients

3 cups kefir (page 41) or yogurt

¼ teaspoon sea salt (optional)

Tools

bowl

large strainer

thin dish towel

wooden spoon

3. Pour the kefir or yogurt into the strainer.

4. Lay a wooden spoon across the top of the strainer.

A linen or thin cotton dish towel works best. It should be a special towel that is used only for making cheese. Do not wash the towel with soap. Put it in a pot of boiling water to sterilize it. Hang it to dry.

5. Tie the ends of the dish towel across the wooden spoon to make a pouch.

6. Let the kefir or yogurt strain for 48 hours. There will be about 2 cups of yellowish liquid in the bottom of the bowl. This is called whey. In the strainer there will be about 1 cup of cream cheese.

7. Put the cheese in a bowl and stir in salt if you like. It will keep for about 1 month refrigerated.

8. Pour the whey into a glass jar. Whey can be used for soaking grains (page 143) and fermenting vegetables (page 126). It will keep for about 6 months refrigerated.

Sweet Cream Cheese
Stir in 2 tablespoons maple syrup or raw honey instead of salt. This tastes yummy on French toast (page 27).

Cottage Cheese

Makes 2 cups

To make cheese from milk, the milk has to be separated first into thick white curds and watery yellowish whey. Remember the nursery rhyme about Little Miss Muffet? What was she eating? It was probably something a bit like cottage cheese. Cottage cheese is just curds and whey that have been gently heated and drained.

Raw milk naturally separates into curds and whey when left at room temperature for several days. This is because raw milk contains friendly bacteria. The friendly bacteria transform the natural sugar in milk (lactose) into lactic acid. This makes the milk taste sour and also causes it to thicken and separate. A culture, like kefir or yogurt, can be added to the milk to make it separate faster.

Ingredients

½ gallon raw milk

1 cup kefir (page 41) or yogurt

½ teaspoon sea salt

Tools

plate

knife

pot

2 large glass or ceramic mixing bowls

spoon

strainer

candy thermometer

1. Pour the milk into a mixing bowl. Cover the bowl with a plate and leave it in the refrigerator for about 24 hours or until the cream rises to the top. Skim off the cream with a spoon and save it in a container in the refrigerator. You will need it later.

2. Add the kefir or yogurt to the skimmed milk and mix with a spoon. Cover the bowl with a plate again and leave it at room temperature until the milk thickens like yogurt. This is called the curd. This will take 1-2 days depending on the temperature in your house and the freshness of the milk.

3. Using a knife, cut the curd into tiny squares by slicing it horizontally, then vertically. Each cut should be about 1/4-1/2 inch apart.

4. Fill a pot with about 1 inch of water. Place the pot on the stove over low heat and set the bowl of curds on top.

5. Measure the temperature of the curds every 5 minutes with a candy thermometer. Then gently stir the curds for a few seconds. Do this until the temperature reaches 110 degrees. This should take about a half hour.

6. Set a strainer over a mixing bowl. Gently pour the curds and whey through the strainer. The curds will stay in the strainer and the whey will run into the bowl below.

7. Rinse the curds with cold, filtered water in the sink. Gently stir the curds until all the water drains out.

8. Put the curds in a container and mix with salt and the cream you saved from skimming. Store the cottage cheese in the refrigerator or find a comfy place to sit and enjoy it while it's fresh and delicious as can be. Just watch out for spiders!

The leftover whey from this recipe is usually a bit cloudy. This whey can be used for soaking grains (page 143) or feeding to your pets, pigs or chickens. If you want to use it for fermenting vegetables, strain it through a dish towel first following the technique used to make cream cheese on page 44.

How is cheese made?
Hard cheeses, like cheddar, are made the same way as soft cheeses, like cream cheese and cottage cheese. First, the milk is fermented. Then the whey is drained off. To make the cheese hard, it is put into a press to squeeze out more whey. The cheese is then aged for several months to allow the texture and flavor to develop.

Cheese made from raw grass-fed milk has all the benefits of raw milk. It is a perfect food, full of protein, healthy fat, minerals, vitamins and enzymes. But unlike milk, cheese is very portable. You can take it with you on a hike or when you travel. Cheese and crispy nuts (page 65) make a delicious on-the-go snack.

Cheese Sauce

Serves 4

There are so many ways to enjoy this savory sauce. Spread it on toasted whole grain sourdough bread to make a "grilled" cheese sandwich. Dip homemade corn tortilla chips (page 72) in it to make nachos. Or drizzle it over cooked vegetables, like asparagus, broccoli or cauliflower.

1. Grate the cheese.

2. Fill a pot with about 2 inches of water. Bring the pot of water to a boil and then turn off the stove.

3. Put the butter and cream in a glass measuring cup. Place the measuring cup in the pot of hot water and stir with a spoon until the butter melts.

4. Add the grated cheese and stir until the mixture is smooth.

5. Mix in the egg yolks and salt. Serve immediately.

Ingredients

2 cups raw cheddar cheese, grated

¼ cup butter (½ stick)

¼ cup cream

2 egg yolks

¼ teaspoon sea salt

Tools

grater

pot

4-cup glass measuring cup

spoon

Butter is Better

Butter is Better

Do you like to eat butter? Almost everyone loves the taste of butter, but some people think the fat and cholesterol in butter is bad for them. So instead of eating real butter, they eat margarine, shortening or spreads made out of vegetable oil. Vegetables are good for us, but do you think "butter" made out of "vegetables" is good for us? Let's explore how vegetable oil and margarine are made to find out…

Vegetable Oil

Vegetable oil includes oils like canola, corn, safflower, sunflower and soybean. These oils are used not only to make margarine, but many other processed foods, including salad dressing, mayonnaise, canned foods, frozen foods, vegetarian foods, chips, cookies and popcorn. How many foods can you find in your pantry or refrigerator with these oils in them? Vegetable oil is also used by fast food places and restaurants to make French fries and other fried foods.

Vegetable oil contains a lot of polyunsaturated fat. Polyunsaturated fat is good for us, because it contains two important nutrients, omega-3 and omega-6 fatty acids. But we need to be very careful with polyunsaturated fat, because it becomes harmful to our bodies when it is cooked or heated at high temperatures.

Unfortunately most vegetable oil is made using a lot of heat. Getting oil out of things like corn, sunflowers and soybeans is not easy. It is done by machines

using heat, pressure and chemicals. The heat damages the polyunsaturated fat and creates something called free radicals. Free radicals hurt the inside of our bodies and can cause cancer and heart disease. When we cook our food in vegetable oil, even more free radicals are created.

Vegetable oils are also unhealthy because most of them contain too much omega-6 fatty acids and not enough omega-3 fatty acids. Although both of these fatty acids are good for us, they are only good when we eat them in fairly equal amounts. Eating too much omega-6 without a balance of omega-3 can cause many health problems.

Margarine

Margarine is made out of vegetable oil. To make liquid vegetable oil into a solid stick like butter, it's *hydrogenated*. Hydrogenation was actually invented to make candles out of oil, not to make food. During hydrogenation, the oil is exposed to heat, pressure and a metal called nickel. The liquid oil then becomes a solid fat, but this process creates more free radicals, bad fats called "trans" fat and other harmful toxins.

During hydrogenation the oil turns a grey color, so it is bleached and dyed with yellow food coloring. It tastes terrible and has very few vitamins in it, so artificial flavors and synthetic vitamins are added. It looks and tastes a bit like butter, but eating it is about as healthy as eating plastic.

Expeller/Cold-Pressed Oils
Some vegetable oils are made without using heat. They are usually called expeller-pressed or cold-pressed. Although these oils are better than oils made using heat, they will still create free radicals if used for cooking. And most of these oils still contain too much omega-6 fatty acids.

Trans fat can cause heart disease, cancer and many other health problems. Some people think trans fat is the same as the saturated fat in butter, because both types of fat are solid at room temperature. But trans fat is actually liquid oil that has been made solid artificially using hydrogenation. The saturated fat in butter is naturally solid and does not cause any health problems.

Butter is Better

Butter is made from one simple, natural ingredient… cream. Cream is the part of milk that contains vitamins A, D, E and K. Butter is especially rich in these vitamins when it is made with cream from healthy grass-fed cows.

You can make butter yourself at home (see page 55). No heat, pressure or chemicals are used, so there are no free radicals, trans fat or other harmful things in butter. Butter is low in polyunsaturated fat so it is safe to use for cooking up to 350 degrees. It contains equal amounts of omega-3 and omega-6 fatty acids. It also contains lauric acid, a fatty acid that protects your body from bad bacteria and fungus.

What kinds of foods do you like to eat with butter? Did you know that eating butter or cream with other foods helps you body absorb nutrients from those foods? Eating butter with bread, oatmeal or rice helps your body absorb minerals from the grains. Eating butter with fish helps your body use the omega-3 fatty acids in the fish. Eating butter with vegetables helps your body convert carotenes in the vegetables into vitamins. Eating butter or cream with fruit and other sweet foods slows down your body's digestion of the sugar in these foods, so you won't get a sugar rush.

But what about the cholesterol and fat in butter? Does that make it unhealthy?

Cholesterol

Many people think the cholesterol in butter causes heart disease. But cholesterol is not a bad thing. Did you know that your brain and other organs are made out of cholesterol? Your body needs cholesterol to be healthy and to heal itself. Just as glue is used to fix something that is broken, your body uses cholesterol to repair itself. High cholesterol isn't caused by eating too much butter, eggs or other foods with cholesterol in them. It's caused by eating foods that hurt our bodies, like vegetable oils. When you eat foods that hurt your body, your body adds more cholesterol to your blood to heal itself.

Fat

Does eating butter make you fat? Although it seems logical that eating fat might make you fat, it's not quite that simple. Everything you eat becomes energy in your body. When your body has more energy than it needs, it stores the extra energy as fat. Foods that create too much energy in your body are foods that digest quickly, like white bread, white rice, sweetened cereal, soda, juice, jam, cookies and candy. These foods give your body a burst of energy that it can't use all at once. Butter, however, and other fats digest slowly. Fat gives your body a slow stream of energy instead of a burst. Eating fat with your food actually slows down the digestion of all your food and gives your body a satisfied, full feeling so you won't overeat.

More Healthy Fats

Butter is one of the healthiest fats you can eat, but it's not the only one…

Lard and Tallow

Fat from pigs (lard), cows or sheep (tallow), ducks, geese and chickens is healthy if it comes from healthy animals. Fat from unhealthy animals usually contains too many omega-6 fatty acids. Lard and tallow are safe to use for cooking, even at high temperatures, like deep-frying.

Coconut Oil

Unlike other vegetable oils, coconut oil contains hardly any polyunsaturated fat, so it is safe to use for cooking up to 350 degrees. Like butter, coconut oil contains lauric acid, a fatty acid that protects your body from bad bacteria and fungus. Organic, extra-virgin, cold-pressed, unrefined coconut oil is best.

Olive Oil

Olive oil is lower in polyunsaturated fat and omega-6 fatty acids than other vegetable oils, but be careful it doesn't get too hot when cooking with it. If the oil starts to smoke that means it's too hot. It's better to use olive oil for making salad dressing and mayonnaise than for cooking. Organic, extra-virgin, cold-pressed, unfiltered olive oil is best and contains the most vitamin E.

Fish Liver Oil

Oil from the livers of fish like cod is an excellent source of vitamins A and D. Take a spoonful every day mixed with warm water or some freshly squeezed orange juice. Avoid fish oils not made from the livers though. They are usually boiled for a long time, bleached and deodorized, and do not contain natural vitamins.

Avocados and Nuts

Avocados and raw nuts are full of healthy fat, vitamins and minerals. Add them to salads and sandwiches or just eat them as a snack. Soaking nuts before eating them (see page 65) makes them easier to digest.

Butter

Makes 1 cup

People have been churning cream into butter for centuries. Butter used to be made in wooden barrels called butter churns. A pole was inserted in the top of the barrel and pumped up and down until the cream turned into butter. Today butter is made using machines, but you can still make it the old-fashioned way using a glass jar. Invite your friends over and have a butter-making party. You can take turns shaking the jar and pressing out the buttermilk.

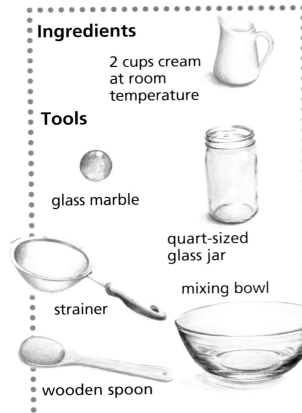

Ingredients

2 cups cream at room temperature

Tools

glass marble

quart-sized glass jar

strainer

mixing bowl

wooden spoon

1. Pour the cream into a glass jar. Drop a marble into the jar and close the lid tightly.

2. Shake the jar for about 45 minutes. First the cream will get thick and you won't hear the marble moving anymore. When the marble starts moving again, you're almost done. Keep shaking the cream until it separates into lumps of butter and a milky liquid. This milky liquid is called buttermilk.

3. Place a strainer over a mixing bowl. Pour the butter and butter-milk into the strainer. The butter-

If you use raw cream, the buttermilk can be saved for soaking grains (page 143). Pour the buttermilk into a glass jar. Leave the buttermilk at room temperature for 8 hours to sour. Then store it in the refrigerator.

milk will flow into the bowl and the butter will stay in the strainer.

4. Remove the marble and transfer the butter from the strainer into a bowl. Cover the butter with cold filtered water. Using a wooden spoon, stir and press the butter against the sides of the bowl to press out more buttermilk. Pour off the water and repeat this step until the water no longer becomes milky.

5. Form the butter into a ball and pat it dry with paper towels. Store the butter in a covered container in the refrigerator.

Butter can also be made in a food processor. Process the cream for about 5 minutes or until it separates into butter and buttermilk. Then continue with straining and pressing out the buttermilk.

Honey Butter Spread

Makes 1 cup

Use this spread to sweeten up whole grain sourdough toast, warm corn tortillas, popcorn (page 74) or cooked carrots (page 96). Bee-licious!

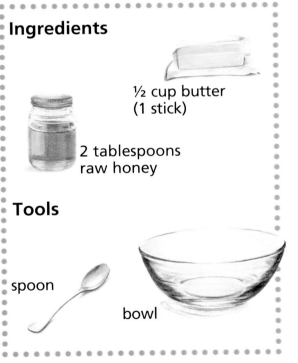

Ingredients

½ cup butter
(1 stick)

2 tablespoons
raw honey

Tools

spoon

bowl

1. Leave the butter at room temperature until soft.

2. Mix the butter and honey together in a bowl.

Clarified Butter

Makes ¾ cup

Butter is mostly fat, but it also contains a small amount of milk protein. The milk protein is what makes butter burn when it gets too hot. If we clarify or remove the milk protein, the butter can be used for cooking at higher temperatures (up to 450 degrees). Clarified butter is also good for making sauces, like Lemon Butter Sauce (page 59), and popcorn (page 74).

Ingredients

1 cup butter
(2 sticks)

Tools

spoon

small saucepan

1. Put the butter in a small sauce-pan.

2. Melt the butter over low heat until it begins to simmer. White foam will rise to the top. This is the milk protein.

3. Using a spoon, carefully skim off the foam.

4. Pour the clarified butter into a jar and store it in the refrigerator.

Lemon Butter Sauce

Makes ¾ cup

This warm, golden sauce makes a perfect dip for fish, seafood or artichokes.

1. Put the clarified butter in a bowl.

2. Put the bowl in a 200 degree oven until the butter melts.

3. Add the lemon juice and mix with a spoon.

Ingredients

½ cup clarified butter (page 58)

juice of 1 lemon

Tools

spoon

bowl

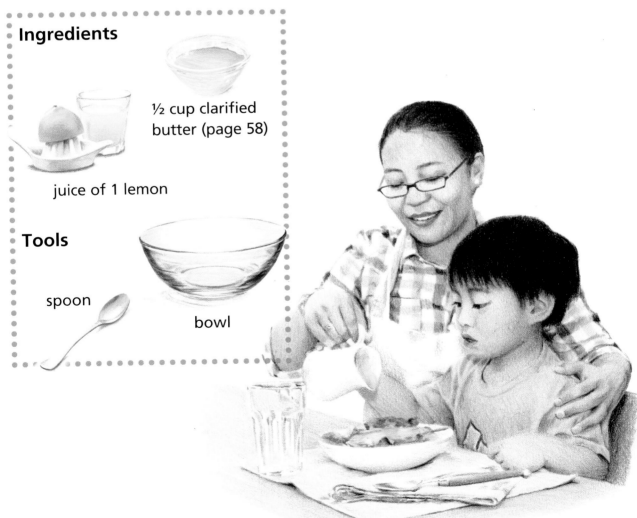

Super Snacks!

Super Snacks!

When your body is growing, it needs a lot of vitamins, minerals, healthy fat, protein and other nutrients. It's important to eat a healthy breakfast, lunch and dinner everyday. If you get hungry in-between meals, eat a healthy snack. Healthy snacks help your body grow super strong.

What is a healthy snack? Nuts, raw milk, cheese, hard-boiled eggs, fruits and vegetables are all healthy snacks. They give your body the vitamins, minerals, fats and proteins it needs to grow.

Are juice and crackers a healthy snack? Juice may be made from fruit, but juice is the sugary part of fruit. Some juices even have sugar added to them. Sugar gives your body energy, but no nutrients to grow. Crackers are usually made with white flour. Like sugar, white flour is an empty food. It fills you up, but it doesn't give your body the nutrients it needs to grow healthy and strong.

Enriched Foods

Many empty snack foods have vitamins and minerals added to them to make them "healthier." They are called enriched foods. But are they really rich?

Whole foods contain many more vitamins and minerals than enriched foods. Whole wheat, for example, contains vitamins B, E and K, calcium, iron, magnesium, phosphorus, potassium, zinc, copper, manganese and selenium. When whole wheat is made into white flour, these vitamins and minerals are removed. When the flour is enriched, synthetic vitamin B and iron are the only nutrients added back in. Vitamins and minerals work together. If some are missing, the others can't do their job.

It's possible there are many nutrients in foods that haven't been discovered yet. Did you know that a hundred years ago, people didn't even know what vitamins were? No matter how much we "enrich" empty foods, we can never match the complexity and richness of whole foods. Eating food whole, the way nature made it, is the only way to be sure your body is getting all the nutrients it needs to be healthy and strong.

Tips for Dehydrating Food

Before canning machines and freezers were invented, how did people keep their food from spoiling? They either fermented it (which we will learn about in another chapter) or dried it in the sun. Bacteria can't grow without water, so food lasts much longer when it is dried.

Many of the recipes in this chapter will instruct you to dry food in a warm oven or dehydrator (an oven designed especially for drying foods at low temperatures). It's best to dry food at a temperature between 100 - 150 degrees. Temperatures above 150 degrees

Toxic Vitamins

The synthetic vitamins added to enriched foods are not the same as the natural vitamins in whole foods. Synthetic vitamins are created in a laboratory and can be toxic to our bodies. For example, synthetic vitamin A can cause birth defects. Natural vitamin A can prevent birth defects. The minerals in enriched foods are also different. For example, the inorganic iron in enriched foods destroys vitamin E. Organic iron does not.

begin to destroy enzymes and vitamins. Temperatures below 100 degrees may not dry the food fast enough to prevent mold.

If the lowest setting on your oven is above 150 degrees, you can still use the oven to dehydrate food, but a dehydrator that keeps the temperature below 150 degrees is better.

Always line the pan you use for dehydrating with parchment paper (also called baking paper). This will protect the pan from getting food stuck to it and will protect the food from becoming contaminated with aluminum, should your pan be made out of this toxic metal. Do not use wax paper or plastic wrap instead of parchment paper. These can melt and stick to the food. And of course never use aluminum foil.

Sugar is a Negative Nutrient
If food were like arithmetic, sugar would be the minus sign. Sugar not only doesn't give your body any nutrients, it actually takes nutrients away! To use the empty calories in sugar, your body needs calcium and other minerals. If it can't get these minerals from your food, it will take them out of your teeth and bones. This is one reason eating sugar causes cavities. Sweet foods should only be eaten in small amounts and with calcium-rich food, like milk.

Crispy Nuts

Makes 4 cups

Did you know that nuts are alive? If you plant a nut in the ground, it will grow into a tree! How does the nut know how to grow into a tree? Do you think the nut has a brain? Some nuts, like walnuts, sure look like brains. Nuts may not have brains, but they do have something special called enzymes. When the nut is put in the ground where it's warm and wet, the enzymes come alive. They transform the nut into a tiny green sprout, which eventually can grow into a huge tree!

Nuts bring new life into the world, just like eggs. Do you think this means they might also be good to eat? Yes! Nuts are full of healthy fat, protein, minerals and vitamins. But the nutrients in nuts are in a form that's hard for our bodies to absorb. This is because nuts are designed to store their nutrients until sprouting time. To release these nutrients, we need to "trick" the nuts into thinking it's time to sprout. One way to do this is to soak them in warm water. The warm water wakes-up the enzymes, just as if the nuts had been planted in the ground. After the nuts are soaked, they can be dried in an oven or dehydrator to make them crunchy again.

Nuts that are prepared this way are called crispy nuts and are much more nutritious and easier to digest than regular raw or roasted nuts. Raw nuts contain irritating substances that may give you a tummy ache. Roasting nuts damages the polyunsaturated fat in nuts.

Ingredients

4 cups filtered water

4 cups raw pecans, walnuts, peanuts, almonds or macadamia nuts

1 tablespoon sea salt

Tools

spoon

bowl

plate

strainer

parchment paper

cookie sheet

When making crispy nuts, it's important to use raw nuts, because the enzymes in roasted nuts are dead. Remember, it's the enzymes that transform the nuts into a more nutritious food. Raw nuts aren't always really raw, however. Sometimes the term "raw" just means "not roasted." Many nuts that are labeled raw are pasteurized, which also destroys the enzymes. It's best to buy nuts directly from a grower, so you can find out whether they are really raw.

1. Put the nuts in a bowl. Add the salt and water and stir with a spoon.

2. Cover the bowl with a plate and leave in a warm place for 7 - 12 hours.

3. Drain the nuts in a strainer into the sink.

4. Line a cookie sheet with parchment paper.

5. Spread the nuts onto the cookie sheet.

6. Place in a warm oven (100 - 170 degrees) or a dehydrator for 12 - 48 hours or until completely dry and crisp.

7. Store in an airtight container. Walnuts should be stored in the refrigerator to prevent rancidity.

Crispy nuts make a super snack with raw cheese. Or grind them up to make nut butter (page 68).

Spiced Pecans

Makes 4 cups

Ingredients

¼ cup maple syrup

3 egg whites

pinch sea salt

2 teaspoons cinnamon

2 teaspoons vanilla

4 cups crispy pecans (page 65)

Tools

spoon

mixing bowl

whisk

parchment paper

cookie sheet

Enjoy these during holidays and at parties instead of chocolate or candy.

1. Put the egg whites in a mixing bowl (see page 34 for instructions on how to separate the eggs) with a pinch of salt.

2. Beat with a whisk until the mixture is foamy.

3. Add the maple syrup, cinnamon and vanilla.

4. Add the pecans and stir with a spoon until all the nuts are coated in the egg white mixture.

5. Line a cookie sheet with parchment paper.

6. Spread the nuts onto the cookie sheet.

7. Place in a warm oven (100 - 170 degrees) for 3 hours or until the egg white coating is dry.

8. Store in an airtight container in the refrigerator.

Crispy Nut Butter

Makes 3 cups

A peanut butter and jelly sandwich makes a yummy snack, but instead of using store-bought peanut butter made from roasted nuts, make your own using crispy nuts! And instead of sugary jelly use apricot butter (page 134), fresh banana or raw cheese slices. Serve on whole grain sourdough bread. Now that's a super PB&J!

Ingredients

4 cups crispy nuts (page 65)

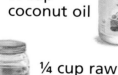
¾ cup coconut oil

¼ cup raw honey

1 teaspoon sea salt

Tools

food processor

1. Grind the nuts in a food processor for about 5 minutes or until a smooth butter forms.

2. Add the coconut oil, honey and salt and process for another minute.

3. Transfer the nut butter to a container and store in the refrigerator.

Carob Nut Butter

Makes 3 cups

Ingredients

4 cups crispy nuts (page 65)

¾ cup coconut oil

¼ cup raw honey

¼ cup carob powder

2 teaspoons vanilla extract

Tools

food processor

This nut butter makes a good substitute for Nutella, without the refined sugar, caffeine or artificial flavors.

1. Grind the nuts in a food processor for about 5 minutes or until a smooth butter forms.

2. Add the coconut oil, carob powder, honey and vanilla and process for another minute.

3. Transfer the nut butter to a container and store in the refrigerator.

Celery Boats

Serves 4

Ahoy, matey! With these celery boats you can pretend you are a sailor or pirate on the high seas. Raisins or buttered blueberries (page 81) can be used as cannonballs. Dried anchovies make great sea monsters. After the boats are blown to smithereens, you get to eat it all up. Anchors aweigh!

Ingredients

2 celery stalks

½ cup crispy nut butter (page 68)

4 slices raw cheddar cheese

Tools

knife

cutting board

1. Cut each celery stalk into 4 pieces.

2. Fill the celery hollows with nut butter.

3. Slice the cheese. Then cut each slice in half diagonally to make triangles. Use the cheese triangles to make sails.

Carrots with Cream Cheese Dip

Serves 4

This snack is easy to remember how to make. All the ingredients start with C (or sea)!

Ingredients

4 carrots

2 tablespoons chopped chives or green onions

¾ cup cream cheese (page 43)

¼ cup cream

½ teaspoon sea salt

Tools

vegetable brush or peeler

fork

knife

bowl

cutting board

1. Peel the carrots or scrub the carrots with a vegetable brush until they are very clean.

2. Slice the carrots into pieces for dipping.

3. Cut the chives into tiny pieces.

4. Put the chives, cream cheese, cream and salt in a bowl. Whip together with a fork.

5. Put the carrots on a plate and serve with the cream cheese dip.

Tortilla Chips

Serves 4

Most chips are fried in unhealthy vegetable oils and flavored and colored with artificial ingredients. Make better chips at home using a healthy fat like coconut oil. Don't forget to make something yummy to dip them in, like guacamole (page 78), salsa (page 135) or bean dip (page 159). Or pour cheese sauce (page 48) over them to make nachos.

Ingredients

4 corn tortillas

2 tablespoons coconut oil

sea salt

Tools

pizza cutter

parchment paper

cookie sheet

1. Preheat the oven to 350 degrees.

2. Line a cookie sheet with parchment paper.

3. Spread the coconut oil on the tortillas and place the tortillas on the cookie sheet, oily-side up.

4. Sprinkle a little salt on top.

5. Cut each tortilla in half using a pizza cutter. Then cut each half into 3 triangles.

6. Bake for 10 minutes. Then turn off the oven and open the door a few inches. Leave the chips in the oven to crisp for another 10 minutes.

Coconut Chips

Makes 2 cups

Ingredients

½ teaspoon sea salt

 ½ teaspoon cinnamon (optional)

2 cups unsweetened dried coconut flakes

Tools

cookie sheet

These are a good on-the-go snack. You can mix them with crispy nuts (page 65) and raisins to make trail mix. If they lose their crunch, just put them back on a cookie sheet in the oven for a few minutes to re-crisp.

1. Preheat the oven to 350 degrees.

2. Spread the coconut flakes into a thin layer on the cookie sheet.

3. Bake for about 5 minutes or until lightly browned.

4. Let the flakes cool completely.

5. Transfer the flakes to a storage container. Add the salt and optional cinnamon.

6. Cover the container with a lid and shake to mix, or mix with a spoon.

Popcorn

Makes 8 cups

Today popcorn is like a space age food made in microwaves, but did you know that popcorn is really an ancient food that people have been making for thousands of years? Native Americans made popcorn in clay pots or by putting sticks through dried cobs and roasting them over a fire. They most likely taught the pilgrims how to make popcorn.

Ingredients

sea salt

3 tablespoons coconut oil

¼ cup popcorn kernels

3 tablespoons clarified butter (page 58)

Tools

spoon

pot with a lid

Here's how to make popcorn the old-fashion way, in a pot on the stove…

1. Put the coconut oil in a pot and add just a few kernels of popcorn. Cover the pot with a lid.

2. Place the pot on the stove over medium heat. Wait until one of the kernels pops. Then add the rest of the kernels.

3. Cover the pot with the lid again, but leave the lid ajar so that steam can escape.

4. Once most of the kernels have popped and the popping begins to slow down, remove the pot from the stove. Wait for the popping to stop. Then pour the popcorn into a serving bowl.

5. Place the butter in the empty, hot pot

and stir it with a spoon until it stops bubbling. Pour the melted butter over the popcorn.

7. Sprinkle salt on top.Mix the popcorn with a spoon and serve.

Snap, crackle, popcorn!
Put some unbuttered popcorn in a bowl. Pour raw milk slowly over the top and the popcorn will go snap, crackle, pop! Eat the popcorn and milk with a spoon.

Microwaves
Making food in a micro wave may be quick and easy, but is it healthy? Studies show that microwaves damage the fats, proteins and vitamins in food, making these nutrients harder for our bodies to digest and toxic to our livers and nervous systems. The ingredients in microwave foods are also not very healthy to begin with. For example, microwave popcorn usually contains partially hydrogenated vegetable oil, artificial flavors, colors and preservatives.

Rice Crackers

Makes 4 dozen

Ingredients

2 cups cooked brown rice (page 154)

2 tablespoons raw honey

2 tablespoons naturally fermented miso or soy sauce

Tools

cookie cutters (optional)

cup

parchment paper

cookie sheet

food processor

Put two of these crackers together with cream cheese (page 43), avocado or smoked salmon in the middle to make a delicious cracker sandwich!

1. Cook the rice following the recipe on page 154. Cut the recipe in half to make 2 cups cooked rice.

2. Put all the ingredients in a food processor and process until the rice turns into a dough.

3. Line a cookie sheet with parchment paper.

4. With clean hands, roll the dough into tiny balls. Set the balls on the cookie sheet, a dozen at a time, leaving a few inches of space around each one.

5. Cover the balls with another sheet of parchment paper.

6. Flatten the balls into

thin rounds using the bottom of a cup. Then carefully peel off the top sheet of parchment paper. If you like, you can trim the crackers into fun shapes using cookie cutters.

7. Put the crackers in a 150 - 170 degree oven or a dehydrator for about 4 hours or until crisp.

Seaweed Crackers

Add 4 teaspoons dried seaweed. Soak the seaweed in warm water to make it soft before adding it to the food processor when you make the dough.

Guacamole

Serves 4

Ingredients

2 ripe avocados

juice of ½ lime

pinch sea salt

Tools

knife

cutting board

bowl

fork

Did you know that avocados are a fruit? They are packed with vitamins, minerals and healthy fat. They are a super fruit!

1. Peel and seed the avocados and put the flesh in a bowl.

2. Sprinkle with lime juice and salt.

3. Mash with a fork until lumpy.

How to Peel and Seed an Avocado
Avocados have a thick skin and a big seed in the middle that need to be removed before you can eat them. First, cut the avocado in half around the seed. Twist the halves in opposite directions to separate them. The seed will stay in one of the halves. Cut both halves in half again. Now you can remove the seed and peel off the skin.

Fruit Snacks

It may say "made with real fruit" on the box, but most fruit snacks are made with fruit juice concentrate (not fresh, whole fruit) and unhealthy ingredients like sugar, corn syrup, partially hydrogenated vegetable oil, preservatives and artificial colors and flavors.

Here are some fruit snacks you can make at home using *really* real fruit. Use local, organic fruit from a fruit stand, farmer's market or your own backyard. Fruit that is fresh and picked when it is ripe contains more nutrients than fruit that is picked early, shipped long distances and artificially ripened (as most fruit sold in supermarkets is).

Fruit Rolls

Makes 4 rolls

Ingredients

2 cups
ripe fruit
(apricots,
peaches,
plums, cherries,
berries, apples,
pears, grapes,
mangos, bananas)

Tools

cutting board

knife

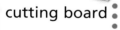

spatula

food processor

parchment paper

cookie
sheet

1. Cut the fruit into pieces. Remove any pits, seeds or stems. There is no need to peel the fruit unless the peel is inedible.

2. Put the fruit in a food processor and blend into a smooth puree.

3. Line a cookie sheet with parchment paper.

4. Pour the fruit puree onto the cookie sheet. Spread into a thin, even layer with a spatula. Try not to spread too close to the edges of the cookie sheet.

5. Place in a warm oven (100 - 170 degrees) or a dehydrator for 12 - 48 hours or until the fruit is no longer sticky in the middle.

6. Leaving the parchment paper attached, roll the fruit up. Cut the roll into 4 pieces. Store in an airtight container in the refrigerator.

7. To eat, unroll and remove the parchment paper.

Buttered Blueberries

Makes 1 cup

Ingredients

3 cups blueberries

3 tablespoons butter

Tools

pot

spoon

parchment paper

cookie sheet

1. Melt the butter in a pot over low heat.

2. Remove the pot from the stove and add the blueberries. Mix together gently.

3. Line a cookie sheet with parchment paper. Spread the blueberries onto the cookie sheet.

4. Place in a warm oven (100 - 170 degrees) or a dehydrator for about 8 hours or until chewy. Store in an airtight container in the refrigerator.

Watermelon Pops

Makes 1-2 dozen popsicles

Ingredients

1 watermelon

Tools

cookie cutters

popsicle sticks

cutting board

knife

parchment paper

cookie sheet

Keep cool during the summer with these super fun easy-to-make pops.

1. Cut the watermelon into 1-inch thick slices.

2. Lay the slices flat on a cutting board. Press the cookie cutters into the watermelon slices to cut out shapes.

3. Line a cookie sheet with parchment paper.

4. Insert popsicle sticks into the bottom of the water-melon shapes. Set them on the cookie sheet and freeze for about 4 hours.

Eat up the leftover watermelon while you wait for the pops to freeze.

Banana Pops
Peel some bananas and cut them in half. Insert popsicle sticks and freeze.

Fruit and Cheese Kabobs

Makes 1 dozen kabobs

Ingredients

1 pound raw cheddar cheese (or any hard cheese)

½ cantaloupe

12 strawberries

12 green grapes

12 black grapes

Tools

knife

melon baller

bamboo skewers

cutting board

Fruit kabobs are a healthy, colorful, fun-to-eat treat for a party or potluck. Adding cheese makes them even more nourishing.

1. Cut the cheese into cubes.

2. Have an adult cut the cantaloupe in half. Remove the seeds with a spoon. Scoop out the melon into balls using a melon baller (or a round measuring spoon will work too).

3. Remove the stems from the strawberries and grapes.

4. Place the fruit and cheese on the skewers following a pattern (such as green grape, cheese, cantaloupe, cheese, strawberry, cheese, black grape).

5. To serve, place the hollowed-out cantaloupe half on a plate with the hollow side down. Then stick the kabobs into the cantaloupe.

Vibrant Vegetables!

Vibrant Vegetables!

Have you ever wondered why tomatoes are red or carrots are orange? Vegetables contain special nutrients called carotenes that turn different colors in the sun. Tomatoes contain a carotene called lycopene. What color do you think lycopene turns in the sun? Red! Tomatoes that get lots of sun while they are growing will have a deep red color. The deep color is also a sign that the tomato has lots of vitamins in it, since sunlight creates vitamins in vegetables too.

Vegetables begin to loose their vitamins soon after they are picked, though, so it's best to eat vegetables when they are fresh. You can tell if a vegetable is fresh by holding it in your hands. If it feels mushy, rubbery or limp, it's probably not fresh. Growing your own vegetables or buying them from a local farm is the best way to get fresh vegetables.

Vegetables are a good source of vitamins and minerals, but they aren't as rich in these nutrients as animal foods, like milk, eggs and meat. It would be very difficult to get all the nutrients your body needs if you ate only vegetables. But vegetables do contain some nutrients that aren't in animal foods, like carotenes and fiber. Carotenes help protect your body from cancer and other diseases. Fiber helps to move waste out of your body. Raw vegetables also contain enzymes that help your body digest food. Vegetables are especially rich in enzymes when they are fermented into foods like pickles and sauerkraut (page 130).

The Dirt on Vegetables
Vegetables can only be as healthy as the soil they are grown in. If the soil is missing nutrients, the vegetables will be missing these nutrients too. If chemicals are added to the soil to kill bugs, weeds and fungus, these chemicals will be in the vegetables too. When animals are fed vegetables grown in unhealthy soil, their meat, milk and eggs will not be as healthy either. Being healthy starts with eating healthy food. Healthy food starts with healthy soil.

Rainbow Salad

Fruits and vegetables come in many different colors. The colors can give us a clue about the nutrients inside. Orange vegetables usually contain the most beta-carotene, a nutrient your body can convert to vitamin A. Green vegetables usually contain more minerals and B vitamins. Red vegetables are high in lycopene, a nutrient that protects your body from cancer.

A rainbow salad is a salad made with fruits and vegetables that are different colors. Rainbow salads are fun to make and contain a wide variety of vitamins, minerals, carotenes and enzymes. The ingredi-

Yellow/Orange

carrot

yellow tomato

bell pepper

jicama

pineapple

Red/Purple

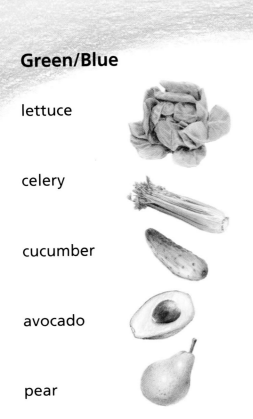

tomato

bell pepper

beet

apple

raisins

Green/Blue

lettuce

celery

cucumber

avocado

pear

ents for this recipe are up to you! To make your salad colorful, pick at least one fruit or vegetable from each color group.

1. Chop or grate the fruit and vegetables into small pieces.

2. Put them in a salad bowl.

3. Drizzle homemade dressing (page 91) on top and mix together with a spoon.

Tools

knife

grater

spoon

cutting board

salad bowl

Add-ins

To make your salad even more delicious and nutritious, you can add chopped crispy nuts (page 65), hard boiled egg (page 23), broken tortilla chips (page 72), croutons (page 121) or bacon cut into bits.

Grated carrot, chopped celery, raisins and crispy nuts

Chopped tomatoes, cucumbers, orange bell pepper and broken tortilla chips

Lettuce, chopped apples, pineapple and bacon bits

Chopped avocado, red and yellow tomatoes and egg

Shake It Up! Salad Dressings

Most store-bought salad dressings are made with unhealthy vegetable oils, artificial flavors and preservatives. Homemade dressing made with olive oil and natural ingredients is much better for you. And it's fun to make when you shake it up in a jar!

Honey Mustard Dressing

Makes ¼ cup

Put all the ingredients in a glass jar. Cover the jar tightly with a lid and shake to mix.

Ingredients

3 tablespoons extra-virgin olive oil

2 teaspoons raw apple cider vinegar or lemon juice

½ teaspoon Dijon mustard

Tools

1 teaspoon raw honey

glass jar

Cream Cheese Dressing

Makes ½ cup

Ingredients

¼ cup honey mustard dressing (page 91)

¼ cup cream cheese (page 43)

pinch sea salt

Prepare the honey mustard dressing. Add the cream cheese and salt. Shake to mix. This makes a great dip for vegetable sticks.

Did you know that the fat or oil in salad dressing helps your body to digest the salad and convert carotenes in the vegetables into vitamins?

Avocado Dressing

Makes ½ cup

Ingredients

1 ripe avocado

¼ cup honey mustard dressing (page 91)

juice of ¼ lime

pinch sea salt

Tools

knife

bowl

fork

cutting board

1. Prepare the honey mustard dressing.

2. Peel and seed the avocado (see page 78 for instructions).

3. Put the avocado in a bowl. Mash with a fork until smooth.

4. Add the avocado, lime juice and salt to the dressing. Shake to mix.

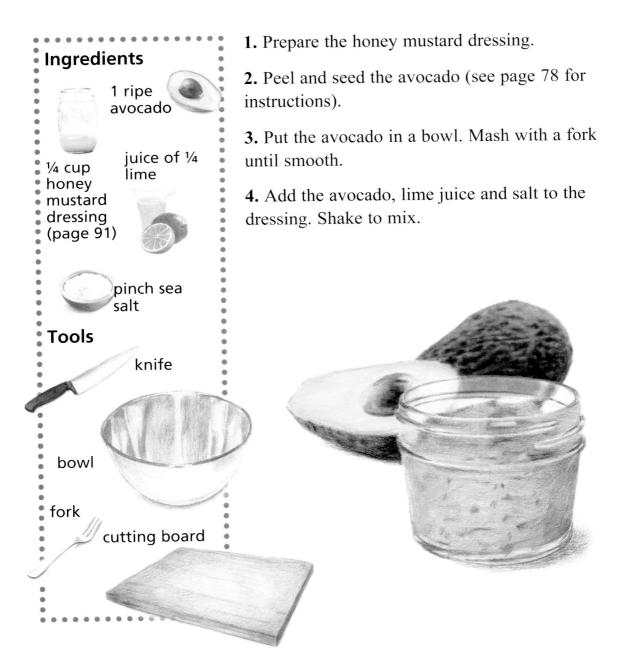

Cauliflower and Cheese

Serves 4

Ingredients

1 large head cauliflower

cheese sauce (page 48)

dash pepper

¼ teaspoon sea salt

2 tablespoons coconut oil

Tools

knife

spoon

glass baking dish

grater

cutting board

Cauliflower turns tender and sweet when it's roasted. Serve it in bowls with cheese sauce for a savory treat. It's like macaroni and cheese, but better.

1. Preheat the oven to 350 degrees.

2. Cut the cauliflower in half. Then cut out and remove the core.

3. Break or cut the cauliflower into bite-sized pieces.

4. Put the coconut oil in a baking dish. If the oil is hard, put the baking dish in the oven until the oil melts.

If you don't have a glass baking dish, a stainless steel baking pan can be used instead. Line the pan with parchment paper.

5. Add the cauliflower to the baking dish and sprinkle with salt and pepper. Mix with a spoon until all the cauliflower is coated in oil.

6. Bake for 30 minutes or until the cauliflower is tender. Tender means it is soft but not mushy. Meanwhile, prepare the cheese sauce.

7. Serve the cauliflower in bowls mixed with cheese sauce.

Carrot Coins

Serves 4

Ingredients

2 tablespoons butter

8 medium-sized carrots

dash pepper

½ teaspoon sea salt

Tools

vegetable brush or peeler

wooden spoon

pot

knife

cutting board

Carrots are fun to grow in a vegetable garden. Did you know that carrots grow under the ground? You can't see them while they're growing, only their leafy green tops show. When you pull them up, it's like finding buried treasure! You can cook them into treasure too, by making carrot coins.

1. Peel or scrub the carrots with a vegetable brush until they are very clean.

2. Cut the carrots into thin round slices.

3. Melt the butter in a pot.

4. Add the carrots and sprinkle with salt and pepper. Mix with a wooden spoon until all the carrots are coated in butter.

5. Cover the pot with a lid. Cook over low heat for about 10 minutes or until the carrots are tender. Stir often so they don't stick and burn.

Bright Broccoli

Serves 4

Ingredients

½ teaspoon
sea salt

2 - 3 heads
broccoli

2 tablespoons
coconut oil

dash
pepper

2 tablespoons
butter

2 tablespoons
water

Tools

knife

large frying
pan or a wok

spoon

cutting
board

Broccoli is very good for you, but it doesn't taste very good when it's overcooked and mushy. The way to cook yummy broccoli is to cook it just until it turns bright green.

1. Cut the heads off the broccoli and break them into pieces that look like little trees. Trim the peels off the stems and cut them into bite-sized pieces.

Optional Toppings: Sprinkle with chopped crispy nuts (page 65) or grated raw cheese.

2. Melt the coconut oil in a large pan over high heat.

3. Add the broccoli, salt and pepper. Mix together with a spoon until all the broccoli pieces are coated in oil.

4. Add the water. Cover the pan with a lid and reduce the heat to medium. Let the broccoli cook for about 10 minutes or just until it turns bright green. Then cook without the lid so the water evaporates, stirring often.

5. Remove the pan from the stove. Add the butter and mix together.

Asparagus Brushes

Serves 4

Asparagus helps to clean the inside of your body, like a brush. Maybe that's why it looks like a brush too. Be careful not to overcook asparagus. Like broccoli, it should be cooked just until it turns bright green.

Ingredients

1 bunch asparagus

1 tablespoon butter

dash pepper

¼ teaspoon sea salt

Tools

tongs

fry pan

1. Cut or break the tough ends off the asparagus.

2. Melt the butter in a fry pan.

3. Add the asparagus to the pan.

4. Sprinkle with salt and pepper.

5. Slide the asparagus back and forth with tongs until all the pieces are coated in butter.

6. Cover the pan with a lid. Cook the asparagus over low heat for 5 - 10 minutes. Thick asparagus will take longer to cook than thin asparagus.

Three Blind Beets

Serves 3

Ingredients

3 medium-sized red or gold beets (gold beets won't stain your hands or clothes like red beets)

2 tablespoons butter or honey mustard dressing (page 91)

Tools

knife

spoon

cutting board

covered casserole

Beets have long thin ends that make them look like mice with tails. Do you remember what happened to the three blind mice? Ouch, they got their tails cut off! When you're cooking beets, it's important not to cut off the "tails" until after the beets are done cooking. Otherwise the sweet juice inside the beets will leak out.

1. Preheat the oven to 350 degrees.

2. Twist the leaves off the beets, leaving about an inch of stem on the beets.

3. Scrub the beets clean with a vegetable brush.

4. Put the beets in a covered casserole and bake for about 1 hour or until you can poke them easily with a knife. Large beets will take longer to cook than small beets.

5. Transfer the cooked beets to a cutting board to cool. Then cut off the "tails" and stems. Scrape off the peels with a spoon.

6. Slice and put in a serving dish. Toss with butter or dressing.

Fresh Corn on the Cob

Serves 4

Ingredients

4 corn cobs

sea salt

butter

Tools

tongs

steamer basket

pot

Corn is best enjoyed in the summer when you can grow it in your own garden or buy it fresh from a produce stand or farmers market. Corn that is eaten the same day it is picked is very sweet and nutritious.

1. Remove the green husks and stringy silk from the corn cobs. Rinse with water to get off all the strings.

2. Fill a pot with about an inch of water. Set a steamer basket inside the pot.

3. Put the pot on the stove over high heat and wait for the water to boil.

4. Add the corn cobs and cover the pot with a lid.

5. Cook over medium heat for 10 minutes.

6. Remove the corn cobs from the pot with tongs.

7. Serve with butter and salt.

The easiest way to put butter on your corn is to roll the corn cob on top of a stick of butter.

Crispy Baked Potatoes

Serves 4

Did you know that most of the vitamins and minerals in potatoes are just under the skin? Peeling potatoes can remove these nutrients, so it's best to eat potatoes with their skins on. This recipe uses oil and salt to make baked potatoes with delicious crispy skins.

Ingredients

4 baking potatoes

sea salt

coconut oil

sour cream or butter

Tools

knife

tongs

fork

vegetable brush

cookie sheet

1. Preheat the oven to 350 degrees.

2. Scrub the potatoes with a vegetable brush until they are very clean.

3. Poke each potato with a fork several times. This will allow steam to escape so the potato won't explode while it's cooking.

4. Rub the potatoes with coconut oil. Then set them on a cookie sheet and sprinkle sea salt all over them.

5. Put the potatoes in the oven directly on the middle oven rack. Put the cookie sheet on a rack below the potatoes to catch any drips.

6. Bake for about 1 hour or until you can poke them easily with a knife.

7. Remove the potatoes from the oven with tongs. Slice open and stuff with butter or sour cream.

Golden Mashed Potatoes

Serves 4

Ingredients

6 medium gold potatoes

drippings from 1 baked chicken (page 176)

½ teaspoon sea salt

1 yellow onion

2 egg yolks

dash pepper

Tools

spoon

potato masher

knife

pot

cutting board

These mashed potatoes are golden because they're made with gold-colored ingredients. They're the perfect side dish for baked chicken (page 176).

1. Wash the potatoes. Then cut them into ½ inch thick slices.

2. Peel and chop the onion into little pieces. (*Store onions in the refrigerator to prevent teary eyes when cutting.*)

To get the drippings for this recipe, bake a chicken following the recipe on page 176. After about an hour of cooking, the chicken will have released most of its juices and you can remove them from the pan with a baster.

3. Put the potatoes, onions, chicken drippings, salt and pepper in a pot. Mix together with a spoon.

4. Put the pot on the stove over high heat.

5. Wait for the drippings to boil. Then cover the pot with a lid and cook over low heat for 30 minutes or until the potatoes are soft.

6. Remove the pot from the stove. Add the egg yolks and mash with a potato masher. Or transfer to a bowl and mash.

Sweet Potato Wedges

Serves 4

Ingredients

2 medium sweet potatoes

sour cream

dash pepper

2 tablespoons coconut oil

1/2 teaspoon sea salt

Tools

spoon

glass baking dish

knife

cutting board

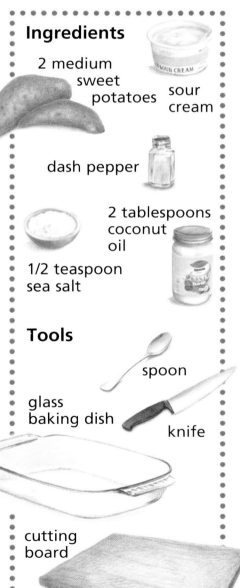

Sweet and sour always go good together, like these sweet potato wedges dipped in sour cream. The healthy fat and friendly-bacteria in sour cream also help your body digest your food. Use real sour cream that is made only with cream and live cultures. Avoid sour creams that contain dry milk powder, starches, gums or other additives.

1. Preheat the oven to 350 degrees.

2. Cut the ends off the potatoes and cut each potato in half. Then, cut each potato half into four wedges.

3. Put the coconut oil in a baking dish. If the oil is hard, put the baking dish in the oven until the oil melts.

4. Add the potato wedges to the baking dish and sprinkle with salt and pepper. Mix together with a spoon until all the potatoes are coated in oil. Then spread the potatoes into a single layer, skin side down.

5. Bake for about 45 minutes or until tender.

6. Serve with sour cream for dipping.

The Secret's in the Soup!

The Secret's in the Soup

What's your favorite kind of soup? There's red tomato soup, orange squash soup and green bean soup. There are clear broths, creamy blended soups and chunky chowders. How do you like to eat your soup? Do you like to slurp it with a spoon? Or drink it in a mug? Maybe you like to dip toast in it.

No matter how you like your soup, there's one secret ingredient that you must not forget. It's something that's white and hard and a dog's favorite treat. Do you know what it is?

It's bones! Bones give soup lots of flavor and nutrients. The hard outside of the bone contains minerals that help your body build strong bones and teeth. Hidden inside the bone is a soft fat called marrow. In Russian, marrow is called "bone brains." Indeed, marrow is very good for your brain and all the organs in your body. The rubbery joints on bones are made of gelatin. Gelatin helps your body digest food better. This means your body will be able to absorb more nutrients from your food.

Bones have so many good things in them, but how do we get these good things into our bodies? Can we chew up a bone like a dog? No, our jaws aren't strong enough for that. A better way is to put some bones in a pot with water and make bone broth…

Bone Broth

Makes 1 quart

Ingredients

bones and scraps from 1 baked chicken (page 176)

1 quart filtered water

1 tablespoon vinegar

2 carrots

½ onion

3 celery

several sprigs parsley

1 bay leaf

Tools

slotted spoon

spoon

knife

strainer

cutting board

large pot

Bone broth is made by simmering bones in water for a long time until the bones begin to dissolve into the water. A little vinegar is added to the water to help the bones dissolve better. This broth is made with chicken bones, but you can also use beef bones or fish bones. Add the chicken head and feet if you have them.

Broth can be eaten plain or made into many different kinds of soup by adding other ingredients. Avoid using store-bought broths that come in cans, powders or little cubes. These are usually made with artificial flavors and are not rich in nutrients like homemade broth.

1. Put the chicken bones in a pot.

2. Add the water and vinegar. The water should cover the bones. If not, add more water.

3. Put the pot on the stove over high heat until the

water comes to a boil. Remove any foam that rises to the top with a spoon.

4. Cover the pot with a lid and lower the heat to a simmer. Simmer for 6 – 12 hours. A simmer means there are bubbles, but the water is not rolling. Add more water as needed to keep the bones covered.

5. Remove the bones with a slotted spoon and wait until they are cool enough to touch. Then break open the bones with your hands (they will be soft and crumbly). Inside the bones you will see the soft marrow or "bone brains." Put the broken bones back in the pot.

6. Chop the onion, carrots and celery into small pieces. Add the chopped vegetables, parsley and bay leaf to the pot.

7. Bring the water to a boil again. Remove any foam that rises to the top with a spoon.

8. Cover the pot with a lid and lower the heat to a simmer. Simmer for 1 hour.

9. Allow the broth to cool completely. Then set a strainer on top of a storage container. Pour the broth through the strainer into the container. Broth will keep in the refrigerator for up to 5 days. To keep it longer, store it in plastic containers in the freezer.

Light or Dark?
This recipe makes a light colored broth. To make a darker colored broth, bake the bones first in a 350 degree oven until well browned.

Coconut Soup

Serves 4

Ingredients

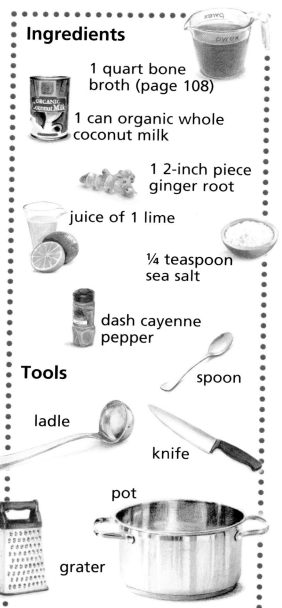

1 quart bone broth (page 108)

1 can organic whole coconut milk

1 2-inch piece ginger root

juice of 1 lime

¼ teaspoon sea salt

dash cayenne pepper

Tools

spoon

ladle

knife

pot

grater

This soup is especially soothing when you have a sore throat or cough. You can drink it in bed in a mug.

1. Put the broth and coconut milk in a pot.

2. Have an adult remove the peel from the ginger root. Then grate the ginger into the pot.

3. Add the lime juice, sea salt and cayenne pepper to the pot. Mix together with a spoon.

4. Put the pot on the stove over high heat until the liquid comes to a boil.

5. Ladle the soup into bowls or mugs.

Chicken and Rice Soup

Serves 4

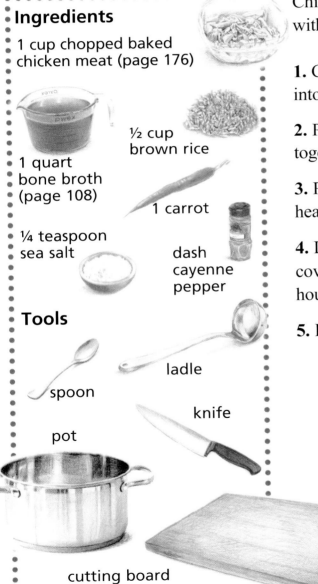

Ingredients

1 cup chopped baked chicken meat (page 176)

1 quart bone broth (page 108)

½ cup brown rice

1 carrot

¼ teaspoon sea salt

dash cayenne pepper

Tools

spoon

ladle

knife

pot

cutting board

Chicken and rice go together so nice with a carrot too, cut into a fine dice.

1. Chop the chicken meat and carrot into small pieces.

2. Put all the ingredients in a pot. Mix together with a spoon.

3. Put the pot on the stove over high heat until the broth comes to a boil.

4. Lower the heat to a simmer and cover the pot with a lid. Simmer for 1 hour.

5. Ladle the soup into bowls.

Tomato Soup

Serves 4

Ingredients

½ onion

4 - 6 roma tomatoes

1 garlic clove

2 tablespoons butter

1 7-ounce jar tomato paste

1 tablespoon dehydrated cane sugar juice

2 cups bone broth (page 108)

¼ teaspoon cumin

¼ teaspoon paprika

½ teaspoon sea salt

sour cream

dash pepper

Tools

ladle

wooden spoon

serrated vegetable peeler

knife

pot

cutting board

1. Peel the tomatoes using a serrated vegetable peeler. Then cut each tomato in half and in half again to make four quarters. Remove the seeds and cores. Then cut the tomatoes into tiny pieces.

2. Peel the onion and garlic and cut them into tiny pieces.

3. Put the onion and garlic in a pot with the butter. Put the pot on the stove over medium heat. Cook, stirring often, until the onion is translucent.

4. Add the tomatoes to the pot and cook until soft.

5. Add all the other ingredients, except for the sour cream, and bring to a boil over high heat. Then cover the pot with a lid and cook over low heat for 30 minutes.

6. Ladle the soup into bowls and serve with a spoonful of sour cream on top.

Butternut Squash Bisque

Serves 4

Bisque (rhymes with "whisk") means a creamy blended soup. This bisque is made with butternut squash. This funny-shaped squash is called butternut because it's smooth as butter and sweet as a nut.

Ingredients

1 butternut squash

2 cups bone broth (page 108)

sour cream

½ teaspoon sea salt

dash pepper

juice of 1 lemon

Tools

knife

pot

food processor or blender

spoon

ladle

glass baking pan

1. Preheat the oven to 350 degrees.

2. Have an adult cut the squash in half.

3. Put the squash in a glass baking pan with the cut sides down. Add ¼ inch water to the pan. Bake for 1 hour.

Sour cream contains friendly bacteria that help your body digest food. These bacteria can't survive in a boiling pot, so add the sour cream after the soup has cooled a bit in the bowl.

4. When the squash is cool enough to touch, remove the seeds with a spoon. Then use the spoon to scoop the flesh out. Put the flesh in a food processor or blender and blend until smooth. Add a little bit of broth if it doesn't blend easily.

5. Put about 3 cups of the blended squash in a pot. Add the broth, lemon juice salt and pepper. Mix together with a spoon.

6. Put the pot on the stove over high heat until the soup comes to a boil. Add a little water if the soup is too thick.

7. Ladle the soup into bowls and add a spoonful of sour cream on top.

A handheld blender can also be used to blend the squash right in the pot! Just put all the ingredients in the pot and blend.

Magic Bean Soup

Serves 4

After Jack chopped down the beanstalk, he must have had a lot of beans. What do you think he did with them all? Maybe he made magic bean soup.

Ingredients

sour cream

½ teaspoon sea salt

2 cups bone broth (page 108)

dash pepper

2 ears corn

3 cups fresh or frozen lima beans

Tools

knife

spoon

ladle

pot

cutting board

1. If using fresh lima beans, remove the beans from their shells.

2. Have an adult slice the corn kernels off the cob.

3. Put the beans, corn kernels, broth, salt and pepper in a pot. Mix together with a spoon.

4. Put the pot on the stove over high heat until the broth comes to a boil. Then lower the heat to a simmer. Cover the pot with a lid and simmer for 15 minutes.

5. Ladle the soup into bowls and add a spoonful of sour cream on top.

Clam Chowder

Serves 4

Clams are very rich in vitamins and minerals, especially iron. Iron helps your body build strong muscles. Did you know that some clams can swim, even though they have no arms or legs? Can you swim without using your arms and legs? That takes some strong muscles!

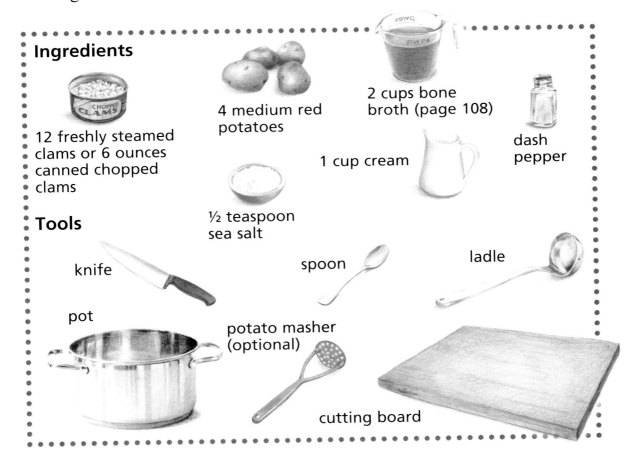

Ingredients

12 freshly steamed clams or 6 ounces canned chopped clams

4 medium red potatoes

2 cups bone broth (page 108)

dash pepper

1 cup cream

½ teaspoon sea salt

Tools

knife

spoon

ladle

pot

potato masher (optional)

cutting board

1. Cut the potatoes into small cubes (there's no need to peel the potatoes).

2. Put the potatoes in a pot with the broth.

3. Put the pot on the stove over high heat until the broth comes to a boil. Then lower the heat to a simmer. Cover the pot with a lid and simmer for 15 minutes or until the potatoes are tender.

4. If using freshly steamed clams, have an adult remove the clams from their shells using a sharp knife and chop them into pieces.

5. Add the chopped clams, cream, salt and pepper to the pot. Mix together with a spoon. To make a thicker chowder, mash some of the potatoes with a potato masher.

6. Bring the chowder to a boil. Then ladle into bowls.

How to Steam Fresh Clams

First, make sure all the clams are closed. Discard any open clams that do not close when touched. This means they are dead and may be spoiled. Put the clams in a bowl and cover with 1 quart filtered water mixed with 1 teaspoon sea salt. Let the clams soak for 1 hour to remove any sand from inside. Fill a pot with 1/4 inch water. Transfer the clams to the pot. Put the pot on the stove over high heat until the water comes to a boil. Then lower the heat and cover the pot with a lid. Steam for 5 – 10 minutes or until the clams burst open. Discard any clams that do not open.

Seaweed Soup

Serves 4

Why are mermaids so beautiful? Maybe it's all that seaweed they eat! Seaweed is rich in a mineral called iodine. This mineral is missing from many foods, because it's often missing from the soil we grow our food in. But the ocean is rich in iodine and foods that come from the ocean, like seaweed and fish, are also rich in this mineral.

Ingredients

4 teaspoons wakame flakes (dried seaweed)

1 quart bone broth (page 108)

2 tablespoons naturally fermented miso

Tools

glass jar

pot

spoon

ladle

1. Put the broth in a pot. Put the pot on the stove over high heat until the broth comes to a boil. Then remove the pot from the stove.

2. Ladle about ½ cup broth into a glass jar. Add the miso and close the jar tightly with a lid. Shake the jar until the miso dissolves.

3. Pour the dissolved miso into the pot. Add the wakame flakes. Mix together with a spoon.

4. Cover the pot with a lid and wait 5 minutes. Then ladle into bowls.

Miso is a traditional Japanese seasoning made from fermented rice, barley or soybeans. Like sour cream, it contains friendly bacteria that help your body digest food. This is why the miso is added to the soup only after removing it from the stove.

Egg Drop Soup

Serves 4

This soup takes teamwork. One person needs to whisk the soup, while the other person pours in the eggs.

Ingredients

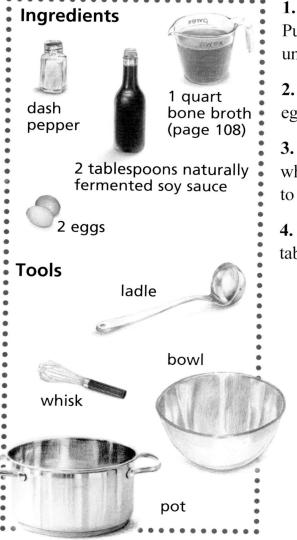

dash pepper

1 quart bone broth (page 108)

2 tablespoons naturally fermented soy sauce

2 eggs

Tools

ladle

bowl

whisk

pot

1. Put the broth and pepper in a pot. Put the pot on the stove over high heat until the broth comes to a boil.

2. Break the eggs into a bowl. Beat the eggs together with a whisk.

3. Slowly pour the eggs into the broth while beating the broth with the whisk to make thin ribbons of eggs.

4. Ladle the soup into bowls and add ½ tablespoon soy sauce to each bowl.

Croutons

Serves 4

Ingredients

4 slices whole grain sourdough bread

¼ cup butter (½ stick)

Tools

fry pan

cookie cutters (optional)

bread knife

spoon

cutting board

Sprinkle these over your soup or salad to add some crunch.

1. Remove the crusts from the bread and cut the bread into cubes. Or use cookie cutters to make fun-shaped croutons for dipping. Save the crusts for making meatballs (page 179).

2. Put the butter in a fry pan. Put the pan on the stove over medium heat.

3. Add the bread to the pan. Cook until crisp, stirring often. For cookie cutter shapes, cook on one side until browned, then turn and cook on the other.

Friendly Ferments

Friendly Ferments

What do yogurt, pickles, sourdough bread, cheese and wine all have in common? They are all fermented foods. They all have a sour flavor too. That sour flavor is created by bacteria. "Bacteria?" you may ask, "don't bacteria make us sick?" Some bacteria can make us sick, but most are actually good for us. In fact, we need bacteria to live. They are our friends, not our enemies.

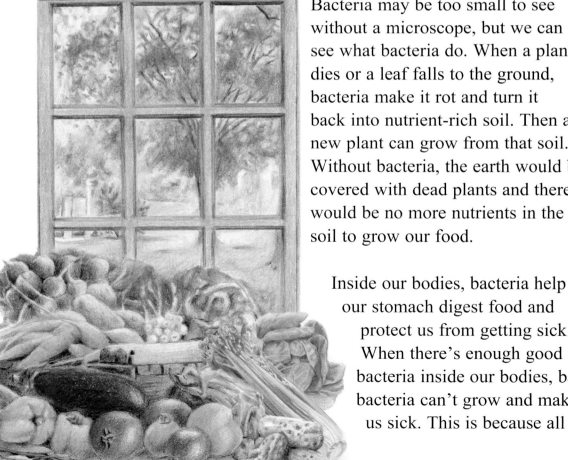

Bacteria may be too small to see without a microscope, but we can see what bacteria do. When a plant dies or a leaf falls to the ground, bacteria make it rot and turn it back into nutrient-rich soil. Then a new plant can grow from that soil. Without bacteria, the earth would be covered with dead plants and there would be no more nutrients in the soil to grow our food.

Inside our bodies, bacteria help our stomach digest food and protect us from getting sick. When there's enough good bacteria inside our bodies, bad bacteria can't grow and make us sick. This is because all bacteria, both good and bad, eat the same thing: sugar. If there's enough good bacteria, the bad bacteria will starve and die. Good bacteria make acids out of sugars, which keep bad bacteria from growing.

To get good bacteria inside our bodies, we need to eat food that has good bacteria in it. Cooked and pasteurized foods don't have bacteria in them, because heat kills bacteria. Only raw and fermented foods have bacteria in them. This doesn't mean we have to eat all of our food raw or fermented. It's still okay to eat cooked foods, like meat, bread and soup. But every meal should include at least some raw or fermented food, like pickled vegetables, sour cream, a salad or a glass of raw milk or fermented soda.

Eating with the Seasons

In the wintertime, it's too cold for most plants to grow. But you can still find lots of fruits and vegetables at the supermarket. Do you know where they come from? They usually come from halfway around the world, where it's summertime. In order to survive the long journey, they must be picked before they are ripe. By the time they arrive at the supermarket, they are old and have very few vitamins left in them.

Before there were supermarkets and before food was shipped around the world, people ate with the seasons. During the winter, there were

not as many foods to eat – usually only root vegetables, grains and animal foods. But people prepared for this. In the summer and fall, when the gardens, orchards and forests were full of fruits and vegetables, they would save the extra by fermenting them. This fermented food lasted many months and could be eaten during the winter.

Fermented foods don't lose vitamins as they get older like fresh foods do. In fact, fermented foods have more vitamins in them than they did when they were fresh. This is because the good bacteria in fermented foods actually make vitamins!

Have you ever wondered why we often get sick during the wintertime? Maybe it's because we're not eating fermented foods during the winter like our ancestors did.

Ingredients and Tools for Fermenting

In this chapter, you will learn how to make fermented fruits and vegetables by a process called lacto-fermentation. Here are a few things you will need before you get started…

Lactobacilli Starter

Lacto-fermented vegetables are made with bacteria called lactobacilli. Lactobacilli live in the soil and on plants, fruits and vegetables. They are also found in raw milk and cultured milk products, like yogurt. It's possible to make lacto-fermented vegetables without adding a lactobacilli starter, since lactobacilli usually live on the vegetables themselves. But if the vegetables have been sprayed with chemicals or washed with soap, they may not have any lactobacilli on them. It's best to add a lactobacilli starter to your ferments. Whey (page 44) and water kefir (page 137) both have lactobacilli in them and can be used as starters. After you've made your first jar of lacto-fermented vegetables, you can simply use a bit of the liquid from that jar (called the brine) as your starter for the next jar.

Mason Jars

You will need quart-sized glass mason or canning jars to ferment the vegetables in. It's best if they have a wide opening. These can usually be found at hardware and kitchen supply stores. It's important to keep the jars tightly closed while the food is fermenting. Lactobacilli do not need oxygen to grow. If air gets inside the jar, other types of bacteria will grow, including the kind of bacteria that makes food rot. Some of the recipes in this chapter will tell you to "burp" the jar. This is to release pressure from inside the jar created by the bacteria giving off air. Unscrew or release the lid just until you hear some air escape, then close the jar tightly again.

Water

Filtered tap water or pure spring water is best. Do not use water that is chlorinated. Chlorine kills bacteria.

Salt

Unrefined sea salt is best. Do not use iodized salt. Iodine kills bacteria. It's very important to use salt when lacto-fermenting vegetables because the salt helps to prevent the growth of bad bacteria before the good bacteria has a chance to grow.

Antibiotics

When bad bacteria makes you sick, your doctor may prescribe an antibiotic. Antibiotics kill the bad bacteria, but they also kill good bacteria. It's very easy to get sick again after taking antibiotics, because your body is left with even less good bacteria to protect itself. You may also get tummy aches, because the antibiotics kill the bacteria that help your body digest food. It's best to avoid taking antibiotics. If you've taken them in the past, eating fermented foods will help put good bacteria back in your body.

Pickled Cucumbers

Makes 1 quart

Ingredients

1 tablespoon mustard seeds

10 – 20 small pickling cucumbers

filtered water

1 sprig fresh dill

1 tablespoon sea salt

¼ cup lactobacilli starter (page 126)

1 cabbage leaf

Tools

quart-sized mason jar

Store-bought pickles are usually pasteurized when they are bottled, which means they no longer have any good bacteria in them. Homemade lacto-fermented pickles are much better. The secret to making delicious crunchy pickles is to use freshly picked cucumbers. Cucumbers sold in supermarkets are not usually fresh enough. Grow your own cucumbers or buy them from a farmer's market. Small cucumbers (about 2 – 3 inches long) will fit more easily in the jar.

1. Put the cucumbers, mustard seeds, dill and salt in a mason jar.

2. Add the lactobacilli starter and enough water to cover the cucumbers, but leave 1 inch of space at the top of the jar. Roll up the cabbage leaf and place it on top of the cucumbers to keep the cucumbers under the liquid.

3. Put the lid on the jar and leave at room temperature for about a week. After a few days, begin "burping" the jar once a day (see page 127). Store the finished pickles in the refrigerator. They will keep for many months.

When the pickles are all gone, remember to save the liquid brine that is left in the jar. You can use it as your lactobacilli starter next time.

Why do pickles make you pucker?
Lactic acid is what makes these pickles and other lacto-fermented foods taste sour. Lactic acid is created by lactobacilli bacteria as they eat the natural sugar in the food. Lactic-acid prevents the growth of bad bacteria, both in the jar and in your body.

Sauerkraut

Makes 1 quart

Ingredients

1 cabbage

1 tablespoon caraway seeds (optional)

1 tablespoon sea salt

¼ cup lactobacilli starter (page 126)

Tools

spoon

knife

kraut pounder (page 223)

quart-sized mason jar

cutting board

mixing bowl

Sauerkraut is made by fermenting cabbage in its own juice. The cabbage is salted and pounded to get the juice to come out. Sauerkraut can be made from green or red cabbage. Can you guess what color the sauerkraut will be if you use both green and red cabbage together? Pink!

1. Remove the outer leaves from the cabbage. Have an adult cut the cabbage in half and cut out the core. Then cut each half in half again.

2. With help from an adult, slice the cabbage into thin shreds.

3. Put the shredded cabbage in a bowl. Add the salt and optional caraway seeds. Mix together with a spoon.

4. Cover the bowl with a towel and leave for 1 hour. During this time, the salt will draw water out of the cabbage and make it easier to pound.

5. Pound the cabbage with a kraut pounder until there is a puddle of juice at the bottom of the bowl. Place the towel under the bowl to keep it steadier while pounding.

6. Add the lactobacilli starter and mix together.

7. Transfer the cabbage to a mason jar. Press down very hard on the cabbage with the kraut pounder until the juice rises to the top. Leave 1 inch of space at the top of the jar.

8. Cover the jar with a lid and leave at room temperature for about a week. After a few days, begin "burping" the jar once a day. Store the finished sauerkraut in the refrigerator. It will keep for many months.

Sweetkraut
After pounding, stir in 2 grated carrots and ¼ cup raisins to make a sweeter kraut.

Pickled Beets

Makes 1 quart

Ingredients

6 – 12 beets

1 tablespoon
sea salt

¼ cup lactobacilli
starter (page 126)

filtered
water

1 cabbage leaf

Tools

knife

peeler

spoon

quart-sized glass
mason jar

cutting board

The deep red color of beets is
nature's way of telling us how good
beets are for our blood and liver. Do
you know what your liver does? It
filters your blood, removing toxins
from your body, which can make you
sick. Your liver also helps your body
digest and absorb vitamins from fats,
like butter and cod liver oil.

1. Have an adult help slice the beets.
First, cut the ends off the beets. Then
peel them. Then cut each beet in half.
Lay the beets flat-side down and cut
them into slices, as thin as possible.

2. Put the sliced beets in a glass
mason jar. Add the salt and lactobacilli starter.

3. Add enough water to cover the
beets, but leave 1 inch of space at the
top of the jar. Roll up the
cabbage leaf and place it on
top of the beets to keep the
beets under the liquid.

4. Put the lid on the jar and leave at room temperature for about a week. After a few days, begin "burping" the jar once a day. Store the finished beets in the refrigerator. They will keep for many months.

When the beets are all gone, save the liquid brine that is left in the jar. You can use it to make Ruby Eggs (page 25) or as a starter for making more pickled beets.

Apricot Butter

Makes 1 quart

This tangy spread can be used in place of jelly or jam. Try it on a sandwich with crispy nut butter (page 68) or with oatmeal (page 148) or pancakes (page 146).

Ingredients

2 cups unsulphured dried apricots

1 cup raisins

2 teaspoons sea salt

1 ½ cups filtered water

¼ cup lactobacilli starter (page 126)

Tools

quart-sized mason jar   spoon

food processor

1. Put the dried apricots and raisins in a mason jar.

2. Mix the water, salt and lactobacilli starter together and pour over the dried fruit. Press down on the fruit with a spoon until the liquid rises to the top.

3. Cover the jar with a lid and leave at room temperature for 2 days.

4. Transfer the contents of the jar to a food processor and blend until smooth.

5. Put the apricot butter back in the jar and store in the refrigerator. It will keep for up to 6 months.

Salsa

Makes 1 quart

Salsa gives food a kick of flavor, and this fermented version makes it easier to digest too. Serve with sour cream and guacamole (page 78), to turn any food into a colorful meal.

1. Remove the skin from the onion. Remove the stem and seeds from the bell pepper.

2. Chop the tomato, onion, bell pepper and cilantro into little pieces using a knife, food chopper or food processor.

3. Put the chopped vegetables in a bowl. Add the tomato paste, lime juice, lactobacilli starter, salt and cayenne pepper. Mix together with a spoon.

4. Put the salsa in a mason jar. Press it down so there is at least 1 inch of space at the top of the jar.

5. Leave at room temperature for 2 days. Then store the salsa in the refrigerator. It will keep for up to 4 months.

Ingredients
1 onion
1 tomato
1 green bell pepper
several sprigs cilantro
1 7-ounce jar tomato paste
¼ cup lactobacilli starter (page 126)
dash cayenne pepper
2 teaspoons sea salt
juice of 1 lime

Tools
spoon
knife
mixing bowl
food processor (optional)
quart-sized mason jar
cutting board

Fermented Sodas

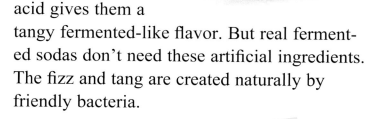

Know Your Ingredients
Can you guess what product this is? The ingredients are: carbonated water, high fructose corn syrup, caramel color, phosphoric acid, natural flavors and caffeine.

It's Coca-Cola. Every 20-ounce bottle contains about 16 teaspoons of sugar (in the form of high fructose corn syrup). Consuming this much sugar at one time can lead to obesity and diabetes. Diet Coke is no better. It's sweetened with aspartame, a toxic chemical that can cause dizziness and depression. The sugar and phosphoric acid in Coke can also cause bone loss and cavities. Because soda is acidic, it leaches the plastic or aluminum container it comes in into the drink. Even when you know how bad Coke is for you, it can be hard to stop drinking it because it contains caffeine, an addictive stimulant like the nicotine in cigarettes.

Did you know that Coca-Cola was originally a fermented drink made with wine? Today cola and other sodas are no longer fermented. They are just made to taste like they are. Carbon dioxide is added to make them fizzy and phosphoric acid gives them a tangy fermented-like flavor. But real fermented sodas don't need these artificial ingredients. The fizz and tang are created naturally by friendly bacteria.

Fermented sodas may contain a small amount of alcohol (usually less than 1%). Dilute with water if necessary. Whey (page 44) can also be used instead of water kefir. Whey will not make a fizzy soda or produce alcohol, but it adds minerals and good bacteria. It makes a refreshing sports drink.

Water Kefir

Makes 3 cups

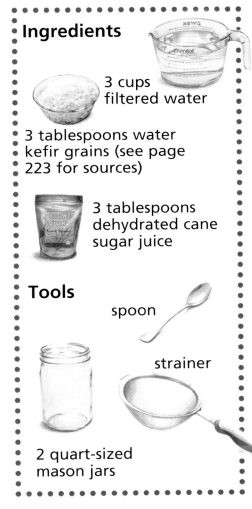

Ingredients

3 cups filtered water

3 tablespoons water kefir grains (see page 223 for sources)

3 tablespoons dehydrated cane sugar juice

Tools

spoon

strainer

2 quart-sized mason jars

Water kefir can be used as a lactobacilli starter for making fermented soda and fermented vegetables. It is made just like milk kefir, except the grains are added to sugar water instead of milk. The grains look like little crystals. If you take good care of your grains, you can use them over and over again. They will grow just like milk kefir grains. Use an unrefined sweetener with natural minerals in it, like dehydrated sugar cane juice (see page 203). The minerals will keep the grains healthy. Honey should not be used, because it is naturally anti-bacterial and can hurt the grains.

1. Put the ingredients in a mason jar and mix together gently with a spoon. Close the jar and leave at room temperature for 2 days.

2. Remove the grains by pouring the water kefir through a strainer into another jar. Close the jar and store in the refrigerator.

3. Put the grains back in the empty jar. Add 3 tablespoons dehydrated sugar cane juice and 3 cups filtered water. Store in the refrigerator until you are ready to make more water kefir.

Grape Cooler

Makes 3 cups

Ingredients

1 cup filtered water

1 cup organic grape juice (not from concentrate)

1 cup water kefir (page 137)

Tools

 quart-sized mason jar

1. Put all the ingredients in a mason jar.

2. Close the jar tightly and leave at room temperature for 2 days or until fizzy. Burp the jar at least once a day. Then store in the refrigerator.

Ginger Ale

Makes 3 cups

Ingredients

½-inch piece
ginger root

1 cup water
kefir (page
137)

juice of
1 lime

2 cups
filtered water

½ tablespoon
vanilla extract

2 tablespoons
dehydrated cane
sugar juice

Tools

grater

quart-sized
mason jar

spoon

strainer

1. Grate the ginger root (there is no need to peel it). Put all the ingredients in a mason jar and mix together with a spoon.

2. Close the jar tightly and leave at room temperature for 2 days or until fizzy. Burp the jar at least once a day. Then store in the refrigerator.

3. To serve, pour the ginger ale through a strainer into glasses.

Coconut Cocktail

Serves 1

Ingredients

½ cup coconut water

¼ cup water kefir (page 137)

Tools

spoon

cocktail glass

1. Put the ingredients in a cocktail glass. Mix together with a spoon.

2. Serve with an orange or pineapple slice.

Soak, Sour
and Sprout!

Soak, Sour and Sprout!

In this chapter, you will learn how to prepare grains and beans in ways that make them easier to digest and more nutritious. Grains and beans can be a good source of vitamins, minerals and other nutrients, but only if they are prepared properly. This is because grains and beans contain things that make them hard to digest like enzyme inhibitors, phytic acid, gluten and complex sugars.

Why do grains and beans contain these things? Because they're seeds! Grain ground into flour makes delicious bread, but did you know that, if planted in the ground, grain will grow into grass? The phytic acid in seeds is there to help the seed store nutrients for sprouting time. It has special "arms" that hold onto vitamins and minerals.

PHOSPHORUS

NIACIN

ZINC

PHYTIC ACID

MAGNESIUM

IRON

CALCIUM

How does a seed know when to sprout? When it is in a moist, warm place, like the ground, enzymes inside the seed wake up and begin breaking down the phytic acid, releasing vitamins and minerals so the seed can sprout and grow.

Where do you think most of the vitamins and minerals are stored in seeds? You might think they are stored inside, but they are actually in the outer layer. The outer layer is the most difficult part of the grain to digest, because it contains the phytic acid and enzyme inhibitors. In grains, the outer layer is called the bran. Removing the bran makes the grain easier to digest. This is how white flour and white rice are made. But removing the bran also removes many of the vitamins and minerals.

A better way to make grains easier to digest, without removing any nutrients, is to soak, sour or sprout them. These methods work by breaking down the phytic acid, enzyme inhibitors, gluten and complex sugars into easier-to-digest parts, just the way nature does when the seed is planted in the ground.

Soaking uses the friendly bacteria and enzymes in cultured milk (like kefir, whey, buttermilk or yogurt) to break down grains into easier-to-digest parts. The grains are ground into flour or rolled, mixed

Enzyme Inhibitors
Have you ever wondered why seeds are often hidden inside sweet and juicy fruits? Although we usually spit the seeds out, animals often swallow the seeds whole and amazingly, these seeds can still sprout and grow into plants after passing through the animal's body. Enzyme inhibitors in the outer layer of the seed protect it from being digested in the animal's stomach. It seems nature has put seeds inside delicious fruits on purpose so they will get eaten (and designed them to be able to survive the journey).

Indeed, it is better for the seed to get eaten, because it ensures the seed will be "planted" in a mound of rich "soil."

with the cultured milk and then allowed to soak for many hours in a warm place so the bacteria and enzymes can do their work.

Souring is like soaking, except a sourdough starter is used instead of cultured milk. A sourdough starter is made by mixing flour and water together and letting it ferment (see page 162). Like cultured milk, a sourdough starter con-tains friendly bacteria and enzymes that break down the grains into easier-to-digest parts. Sourdough bread is made by souring.

Sprouting makes grains and beans easier to digest by allowing enzymes inside to naturally break them down into easier-to-digest parts. Grains and beans don't have to be planted in the ground to sprout. To sprout them for eating, they can be soaked in water, drained and then kept warm and moist for several days. Sprouting is a good way to prepare beans, rice and other grains that are usually eaten whole. Grains that have been ground into flour cannot sprout. While soaking and souring give grains a sour flavor, sprouting makes them sweeter. It also makes them richer in vitamins.

A warm place is needed when soaking, souring and sprouting because bacteria and enzymes are most active when they are warm. Can you think of any places in your kitchen or home that might be warm? If you have a gas oven with a pilot light, the inside of the oven will be warm. Leaving the light turned on inside the oven will also make it warm. Or if you have a microwave oven above your stove with a light on the bottom, leaving the light on will make it warm inside. Other places in your home that might be warm are next to a water heater, fireplace, computer or other appliance that gives off heat.

SOAK, SOUR AND SPROUT

(Sing to the tune of "Shake, Rattle and Roll.")

Get outta that bed
Wash your face and hands;
Get in that kitchen
Rattle those pots 'n pans!
I hope you soured that dough,
'cause I'm a hungry man!

I said soak, sour and sprout!
Come on soak, sour and sprout!
You better soak, sour and sprout!
Come on soak, sour and sprout!
Let those enzymes get
the phytic acid out!

Pancakes

Serves 4

Ingredients

1 ½ cups whole grain flour

1 cup kefir (page 41), whey (page 44), buttermilk (page 56) or yogurt

½ teaspoon sea salt

2 eggs

½ teaspoon baking soda

butter

Tools

grain mill (optional)

mixing bowl

wire whisk

spoon

fry pan

spatula

Have you ever mixed baking soda and vinegar together to make a volcano? These pancakes are made the same way. When flour is soaked or soured, it becomes acidic like vinegar. Adding baking soda creates a chemical reaction that makes the batter bubbly. It's not quite as dramatic as a volcano, but it sure makes delicious fluffy pancakes.

Is your flour fresh?
Unlike white flour, whole grain flour contains oils that turn rancid when the flour gets old. Most flour sold in stores is not very fresh. It's best to buy whole grains and grind them into flour at home using a grain mill (see page 223 for recommended grain mills). Always store whole grain flour in the refrigerator to keep it fresher.

1. If using a grain mill to make fresh flour, grind 1 cup grain to make 1½ cups flour.

2. Put the flour and cultured milk

in a mixing bowl and mix together with a spoon. Cover the bowl with a towel or plate and leave in a warm place for 8 - 24 hours.

3. Put a fry pan on the stove over medium heat.

4. While the pan is heating, add the eggs and salt to the batter and mix together with a whisk. Then sprinkle in the baking soda while whisking the batter. Add some milk or water if the batter is too thick.

5. Melt some butter in the pan to keep the pancakes from sticking. Then, using a ¼ cup measuring cup, pour some batter into the pan to make a pancake. Wait until the edges of the pancake are firm and the bottom is lightly browned, then flip it over using a spatula. Wait until the other side is lightly browned, then transfer it to a plate. Repeat this step, adding more butter as needed, to make more pancakes until all the batter is gone. You can make several pancakes at a time if your pan is large enough.

6. Serve with lots of butter and a natural sweetener, like maple syrup, apricot butter (page 134) or sweet cheese (page 44).

Blueberry Pancakes
Drop blueberries on top of the batter after pouring it in the pan. Try making a smiley face or a heart with them!

Sourdough Pancakes
Add ½ cup sourdough starter (page 162) to the flour when soaking. Fresh milk or water can be used instead of cultured milk.

Oatmeal

Serves 4

Ingredients

1 cup
rolled oats

2 cups filtered
warm water

butter

2 tablespoons
kefir (page 41),
whey (page 44),
buttermilk (page
56) or yogurt

¼ teaspoon
sea salt
(optional)

Tools

spoon

bowl

pot

Use old-fashioned rolled oats, not quick cooking or instant, or better yet, grind your own from whole oat groats. Grind 2/3 cup oat groats to make 1 cup ground oats.

1. Put the rolled oats in a bowl. Add 1 cup warm water and the cultured milk. Mix together with a spoon. Cover the bowl with a towel or plate and leave in a warm place for 8 - 24 hours.

2. Transfer the oats to a pot. Add 1 cup water and the optional salt and mix together.

3. Put the pot on the stove over high heat until the oatmeal comes to a boil. Then cover the pot with a lid and turn the heat down to the lowest setting. Cook for 2-3 minutes.

4. To make the oatmeal thicker, leave it in the pot for about a half hour before serving. Serve with lots of butter and a natural sweetener, like raw honey, maple syrup, apricot butter (page 134) or sliced banana.

Sourdough Oatmeal

Use 2 tablespoons sourdough starter (page 162) instead of cultured milk.

Oat groats or steel-cut oats can be used instead of rolled oats. Grind oat groats in a grain mill on a coarse setting. They will take longer to cook than rolled oats. Increase the water to 3 cups and cook for 30 minutes.

Oat Crunchies

Makes 3 cups

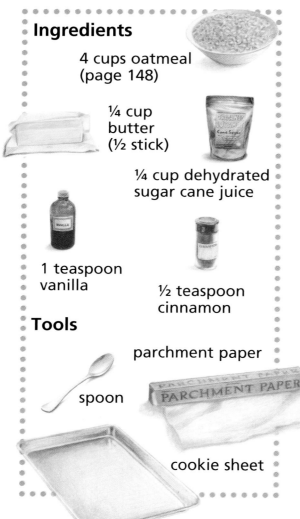

Ingredients

4 cups oatmeal
(page 148)

¼ cup
butter
(½ stick)

¼ cup dehydrated
sugar cane juice

1 teaspoon
vanilla

½ teaspoon
cinnamon

Tools

spoon

parchment paper

cookie sheet

When you're in a crunch for time, these oat crunchies make a quick and healthy breakfast or snack. Serve in a bowl with raw milk. Raisins or banana slices make it even yummier.

1. Make the oatmeal following the recipe on page 148. Double the recipe to make 4 cups of oatmeal.

2. While the oatmeal is still warm, add the butter and the other ingredients. Mix together with a spoon.

3. Line a cookie sheet with parchment paper. Spread the oats into a thin layer on the parchment paper. Bake in a 150 - 170 degree oven or a dehydrator for about 12 - 24 hours or until crisp.

4. Let the oats cool. Then break into pieces with your hands. Store in an airtight container.

Breakfast cereals might be made with whole grains, but the grains haven't been soaked, soured or sprouted. They are made into little flakes and shapes in big machines using heat and pressure. This destroys vitamins in the grains, turns the oils rancid and makes some of the proteins toxic. The cereal is sprayed with synthetic vitamins and minerals to make it appear nutritious on the label, but these "airbrushed" nutrients are difficult for our bodies to absorb. You may just want to say "cheerio" to your Cheerios.

Banana Bread

Makes 1 loaf

Ingredients

½ cup butter (1 stick)

2 cups spelt or whole wheat pastry flour

½ cup kefir (page 41), whey (page 44), buttermilk (page 56) or yogurt

2 eggs

3 very ripe bananas

¼ cup dehydrated cane sugar juice

1 teaspoon vanilla extract

½ teaspoon baking soda

½ teaspoon cinnamon

¼ teaspoon nutmeg

pinch cloves

¼ teaspoon ginger

pinch sea salt

Tools

spoon

whisk

grain mill (optional)

loaf pan

mixing bowl

Mushy bananas covered in black and brown spots may not look very good to eat, but the spots just mean they are very ripe and sweet. Mash them up with soaked flour, eggs and spices and bake in the oven to make the most delicious treat!

1. Put the butter in a mixing bowl. Put the bowl in a warm oven until the butter is soft.

2. If using a grain mill to make fresh flour, grind 1 ⅓ cup spelt or soft white wheat berries to make 2 cups flour.

3. Add the flour and cultured milk to the softened butter. Mix together with a spoon. Cover the bowl with a towel or plate and leave in a warm place for 8 - 24 hours.

4. Add all the other ingredients to the soaked dough. Mix together with a whisk until smooth.

5. Rub butter on the inside of a loaf pan, then transfer the dough to the loaf pan.

6. Bake in a 350 degree oven for about an hour.

Banana Muffins
Spoon the dough into baking cups set in a muffin tin. Bake for about 30 minutes.

Toothpick Test
How do you know if the bread is done? Insert a toothpick in the center. If it comes out clean or with only a few crumbs on it, the bread is done! If there is gummy batter stuck to it, put the bread back in the oven for another 5-10 minutes and then re-test.

Zucchini Bread
Use 1 ½ cups grated zucchini instead of bananas. Add an extra ½ cup dehydrated cane sugar juice.

Brown Rice

Serves 8

Rice is easier to digest than other grains because it is gluten-free and low in phytic acid. Rice can be prepared simply by cooking it in broth and butter, no soaking is necessary. However, if you want to make the rice more digestible, you can sprout it first (page 155).

Ingredients

2 cups brown rice

2 cups filtered water

2 cups bone broth (page 108)

¼ cup butter (½ stick)

1 teaspoon sea salt

Tools

spoon

pot

1. Put all the ingredients in a pot. Mix together with a spoon. Put the pot on the stove over high heat. Let the rice boil uncovered for about 15 minutes or until the liquid is the same level as the rice.

2. Cover the pot with a lid and turn the heat down to the lowest setting. Cook for 1 hour.

Mexican Rice

Add 1 chopped onion, 2 tablespoons tomato paste, ½ teaspoon ground cumin and a dash of cayenne pepper.

Coconut Rice

Instead of bone broth and butter, use 1 can organic whole coconut milk.

Southern Rice

Add 1 cup fresh or frozen lima beans and ¼ cup chopped raisins. Lima beans do not need to be soaked before cooking unless they are dried.

Sprouted Brown Rice

Serves 8

Ingredients

2 cups short grain brown rice

1 teaspoon sea salt

filtered water

¼ cup butter (½ stick)

2 cups bone broth (page 108) or water

Tools

strainer

spoon

bowl

pot

Short grain brown rice sprouts better than long grain, because the grains are more likely to be unbroken. Broken grains will not sprout. Cook the rice as soon as it sprouts. If the sprouts grow too long they will make the rice bitter.

1. Put the rice in a bowl. Add 4 cups filtered water. Leave in a warm place for 8 - 12 hours.

2. Put a strainer in the sink. Pour the rice into the strainer. Rinse the rice with filtered water. Then set the strainer (with the rice inside) on top of the bowl. Cover with a damp towel and leave in a warm place for 12 - 24 hours or just until tiny white sprouts begin to show. Rinse the rice with water every 12 hours to keep it moist.

3. To cook, put the sprouted rice in a pot. Add the bone broth, butter and salt. Mix together with a spoon.

4. Put the pot on the stove over high heat until the broth is boiling. Then cover the pot with a lid and turn the heat down to the lowest setting. Cook for 1 hour.

Sprouted Beans

Makes 6 cups

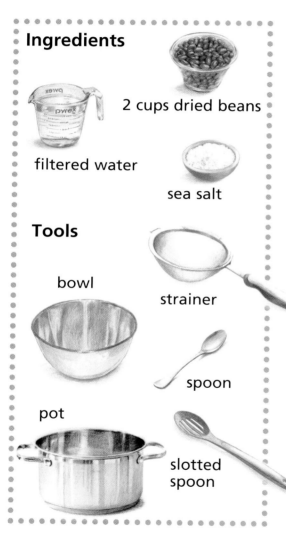

Ingredients

2 cups dried beans

filtered water

sea salt

Tools

bowl

strainer

spoon

pot

slotted spoon

Beans contain a complex sugar called oligosaccharide that our bodies can't digest. This is why eating beans can make you gassy. Sprouting beans before cooking them breaks down this complex sugar into a simple sugar that is easy to digest. Be sure to cook the beans as soon as they sprout. If the sprouts grow too long they will make the beans bitter.

Dried beans last a long time, but the fresher the beans are, the better they will be when cooked. Old beans don't cook evenly (some will be hard while others will be mushy). It's best to buy beans in a sealed package with a date on it instead of from a bulk bin.

1. Put the beans in a bowl. Add 4 cups filtered water. Leave in a warm place for 8 - 12 hours.

2. Put a strainer in the sink. Pour the beans into the strainer. Rinse the beans with filtered water. Then set the strainer (with the beans inside) on top of the bowl. Cover with a damp towel and leave in a warm place for 12 - 24 hours or just until tiny white sprouts begin to show. Rinse the beans with water every 12 hours to keep them moist.

3. To cook, put the beans in a pot. Add water until the beans are covered. Put the pot on the stove over high heat until the water boils. Use a spoon to remove any foam that rises to the top. Cover the pot with a lid and turn the heat down to the lowest setting. Cook for about 1 hour or just until the beans are soft enough to squish between your tongue and the roof of your mouth.

4. Transfer the beans to a storage container using a slotted spoon. To serve, sprinkle with sea salt or make into refried beans (page 158) or bean dip (page 159).

Grow a Beanstalk
If you plant a sprouted bean in a pot of soil, you can watch it grow into a plant. Be sure to put it in a warm, sunny spot (a windowsill is a good place) and keep the soil moist.

Refried Beans

Serves 4

Ingredients

2 cups sprouted and cooked pinto beans (page 156)

¼ cup lard, butter or coconut oil

½ teaspoon sea salt

Tools

potato masher

pot

spoon

Roll these beans up in corn tortillas with grated raw cheese and sour cream to make mini burritos.

1. Put the beans in a pot. Mash the beans with a potato masher.

2. Add the lard and salt.

3. Put the pot on the stove over medium heat. Stir the beans with a spoon until the lard melts and mixes together with the beans. If the beans seem too thick, add a little broth or water.

Bean Dip (Hummus)

Makes 3 cups

Ingredients

3 cups sprouted and cooked garbanzo or navy beans (page 156)

1 clove garlic

juice of 2 lemons

½ cup extra-virgin olive oil

1 teaspoon sea salt

dash cayenne pepper

Tools

food processor

This makes a satisfying snack with tortilla chips (page 72) or whole wheat pita bread. Or spread it on a sandwich like mayonnaise.

Put all the ingredients in a food processor. Blend until smooth. Store in the refrigerator.

Baked Beans

Serves 8

These beans are soaked and then baked very slowly in the oven. Slow-baking beans makes them easier to digest too. Baked beans are delicious with brown rice (page 154) or stuffed inside a baked potato (page 101) with sour cream.

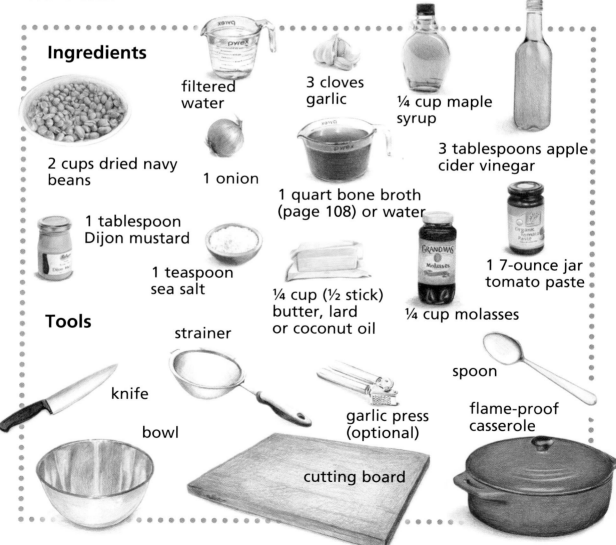

Ingredients

2 cups dried navy beans

filtered water

1 onion

3 cloves garlic

1 quart bone broth (page 108) or water

¼ cup maple syrup

3 tablespoons apple cider vinegar

1 tablespoon Dijon mustard

1 teaspoon sea salt

¼ cup (½ stick) butter, lard or coconut oil

¼ cup molasses

1 7-ounce jar tomato paste

Tools

knife

strainer

bowl

cutting board

garlic press (optional)

spoon

flame-proof casserole

1. Put the beans in a bowl. Add 4 cups filtered water. Leave in a warm place for 8 - 12 hours.

2. Put a strainer in the sink. Pour the beans into the strainer. Rinse the beans with filtered water.

3. Put the beans in a casserole and add the bone broth. Put the casserole on the stove over high heat until the broth comes to a boil. Use a spoon to remove any foam that rises to the top.

4. Peel the onion and garlic, then chop them into small pieces. If you have a garlic press, you can crush the garlic instead of chopping it.

5. Add all the remaining ingredients to the casserole and mix together with a spoon.

6. Cover the casserole with a lid and bake in a 250-degree oven for about 6 hours. Stir the beans occasionally and add more broth or water as needed to keep the beans from burning.

Sourdough Starter

Makes 1 1/2 cups

Ingredients

1 1/2 cups rye or whole wheat flour

1 cup filtered water

Tools

rubber band

spoon

quart-sized glass jar

grain mill (optional)

A sourdough starter is made by mixing flour and water together and letting it ferment for many days. This fermented flour becomes full of friendly bacteria, yeasts and enzymes that are able to break down grains into easier-to-digest parts. You only need to go through the process of making a sourdough starter once. Once made, it will last for as long as needed if fresh flour and water are added regularly.

Freshly ground flour is best because it's full of enzymes. It's difficult to make a sourdough starter from old or store-bought flour. Rye flour makes an especially good starter because it is high in phytase. Phytase is an enzyme that breaks down phytic acid.

1. If using a grain mill to make fresh flour, grind 1 cup grain to make 1 ½ cups flour.

2. Put 1 ½ tablespoons flour and 1 tablespoon water in a glass jar. Mix together with a spoon. Close the jar with a lid and leave at room temperature.

3. Feed the starter 1 ½ tablespoons flour and 1 tablespoon water every 12 hours for 4 days. Try to get lots of air into the starter when mixing it. This encourages the growth of bacteria in the starter.

4. After 4 days, remove half of the starter and discard. Continue feeding the starter 1 ½ tablespoons flour and 1 tablespoon water every 12 hours for another 4 days. After you feed the starter, put a rubber band around the jar to mark the top of the starter. Check the starter a few hours later to see if it has grown above the rubber band. If the starter is growing after each feeding, then your starter is ready to use! If it's not growing after 8 days, discard the starter and try again.

Caring for Your Starter
A sourdough starter is like a pet (some people even give their starter a name). If kept at room temperature, your starter needs to be fed flour and water every 12 hours to keep it alive. If kept in the refrigerator, it only needs to be fed once a week. Keep your starter small. The smaller it is, the less food it will need. ½ cup starter needs to be fed 3 tablespoons flour and 2 tablespoons water at each feeding. It will double in size after only 2 feedings and then it will need to be fed twice as much. When the starter gets too big, use the extra in a recipe or discard some to your compost pile. Storing your starter in the refrigerator is best if you will not be using it often.

Using Your Starter in Recipes
Remember to always save a little bit of the starter. If the recipe calls for 1 cup of starter, you'll need to have at bit more than 1 cup on hand. You can make your sourdough starter bigger quickly by feeding it up to 3 times it's size. That means if you have 1 cup starter, you can feed it up to 3 cups flour and 2 cups water. Wait at least 4 hours after feeding your starter before using it in a recipe.

Sourdough Rye Bread

Makes 1 loaf

Ingredients

1 cup sourdough starter (page 162)

3 cups rye flour

1 cup filtered water

2 tablespoons honey

1 teaspoon sea salt

butter or coconut oil

Tools

spoon

mixing bowl

grain mill (optional)

loaf pan (9" x 5")

This moist, chewy bread is not only easy to digest, but surprisingly easy to make too. Usually bread must be kneaded to make the gluten stretchy so the bread can rise. But rye has a lot less gluten in it than other grains and doesn't need to be kneaded. Instead of gluten, it has stretchy polysaccharides in it that allow it to rise. If you think you don't like rye bread, it may be because you've only tasted the kind with caraway in it. Rye without caraway doesn't taste much different from wheat.

1. If using a grain mill to make fresh flour, grind 2 cups grain to make 3 cups flour.

2. Mix the flour, sourdough starter and water together in a bowl. The dough will be very thick and sticky. If it's too thick to mix with a spoon, add a bit more water or mix together with your hands.

3. Cover the bowl with a damp towel to keep the dough moist. Leave in a warm place for 4 - 12 hours.

4. Add the honey and salt to the dough and mix together. Rub butter or coconut oil on the inside of a loaf pan to keep the bread from sticking. Then transfer the dough to the pan.

5. Cover the pan with a damp towel and leave in a warm place for 4 - 12 hours or until the dough rises to the top of the pan.

6. Bake the bread in a 350-degree oven for 1 hour. When the pan is cool enough to touch, slide a knife around the inside edge of the pan to release the bread. Remove the bread from the pan and turn it upside down to cool. Wait until it has cooled completely before slicing.

Meet Your Meat

Meet Your Meat

Do you know where your meat comes from? Fast-food restaurants serve millions of hamburgers and chicken nuggets everyday, but when was the last time you actually saw a cow or a chicken? Where does all this meat come from?

Most meat comes from animals raised on factory farms. Factory farms don't look like farms at all. The animals get very little sunshine, fresh air or exercise because they are kept inside cages or buildings. Sometimes they are so crowded together, they can hardly turn around. Factory farms feed their animals corn and soy to fatten them up, but these foods are not very good for them. The animals get sick often and because disease spreads so quickly on factory farms, they must be given antibiotics.

Do you know where the fish you eat comes from? At least half of all fish eaten comes from aquafarms, which are like factory farms, just underwater. The fish are crowded into tanks and fed corn and soy like land animals. Do corn and soy sound like natural foods for fish to eat? Have you ever seen corn and soy growing in the ocean? Of course not! In the wild, fish eat plankton, algae and other fish. Farmed fish aren't as healthy for us to eat as wild fish. They have lower amounts of vitamins, minerals and omega-3 fatty acids in them. In fact, farmed salmon aren't even the same color as wild salmon. The farms use a chemical to make the fish pink like wild salmon.

Meat is supposed to be a life-giving food. An animal gives up its life so that we can eat and live. But the meat from animals on factory farms doesn't give life to anyone. The animals have miserable, unhealthy lives and their death only brings more misery, because when we eat meat from unhealthy animals it makes us unhealthy too.

Should we stop eating meat so that animals won't have to suffer on factory farms anymore? Should we stop eating milk and eggs too? Animals certainly shouldn't have to suffer so we can eat, but is becoming a vegetarian or vegan the only solution? It's very difficult to get all the nutrients your body needs, eating only plant foods.

Giving Thanks
Does it make you sad that an animal has to die so you can eat meat? Do you think you could eat meat from an animal you raised or hunted? It would be very different from ordering a hamburger at a drive-thru. Most of us don't like to be reminded that our burger was once a cow with big brown eyes. But is it right to eat meat without remembering the animal's sacrifice? Praying or "giving thanks" before eating is one way to honor and thank the animal (and the Creator) for giving us its life. We can also show honor by not wasting any part of the animal, eating not only the muscle meat, but using the fat, organs and bones too. If we eat the whole animal, then fewer animals have to die. The fat, organs and bones of animals are actually richer in vitamins and minerals than the muscle meat. When you cook meat, always save the drippings in the bottom of the pan. You can use them to make a nutritious sauce for the meat. Organ meats can be ground up and mixed with muscle meats to make meatballs and hamburgers. Bones can be used to make broth for soups and stews.

Where did people get their meat before there were factory farms? They either hunted and fished for wild animals or they raised their own animals on small family farms. Would you like to have your own farm? If you did, you could give the animals everything they need to be happy and healthy. You could raise them on sunny, green pastures where the cows could eat grass and the chickens could eat bugs and worms. Manure is always a problem on factory farms, it smells horrible and has to be cleaned up and hauled away, but when animals are raised on pastures, the manure just goes back into the earth and helps more grass to grow. It also attracts bugs for the chickens to eat. And it can be used as fertilizer for growing fruits and vegetables too. On family farms, nothing is wasted. Food scraps can be composted and used as fertilizer or fed to the chickens and pigs, who in return, give the family eggs and meat to eat.

Even if you can't have your own farm, you can still help stop the suffering of animals on factory farms. You can choose to only buy meat from farms with happy, healthy animals that are raised on pastures and to only buy wild fish that is caught from oceans and rivers. You can choose to buy eggs, milk, cheese and butter from happy, healthy pastured animals too.

Tofu
Is tofu a good substitute for meat? Tofu is made out of soy beans. Because beans are a seed, they need to be prepared properly to be healthy for us to eat. When soy is fermented into foods like tamari (soy sauce), natto and tempeh, it's okay to eat, but not when it is made into tofu. Because of the phytoestrogens and other toxins in soy, it should never be eaten in large amounts as a replacement for animal foods. The traditional way to eat soy, as Asian cultures do, is in small amounts as a condiment with food. Indeed, when soy is prepared properly, it develops a strong fermented flavor that makes it difficult to eat in large amounts.

Teriyaki Fish

Serves 4

Ingredients

1 clove garlic

1 pound wild fish filets

butter

2 tablespoons honey

2 tablespoons naturally fermented soy sauce

pastry brush

small bowl

grater

fork

glass baking dish

Before you say you don't like fish, try it the Japanese way. Oishii! (That means delicious in Japanese). People eat lots of fish in Japan because their country is an island, surrounded by the ocean. They are also one of the healthiest people in the world. Do you think that might be because they eat so much fish?

1. Preheat the oven to 250 degrees.

2. Rub butter on the inside of a glass baking dish. Put the fish skin-side down in the baking dish.

3. Grate the garlic into a small bowl. Add the soy sauce and honey. Mix together with a fork.

4. Spread the sauce on top of the fish using a pastry brush. Then bake the fish in the oven for about 45 minutes or until it flakes easily with a fork.

5. To thicken the sauce before serving, transfer the sauce to a small fry pan and boil for a few minutes, stirring often.

Pan~Fried Fish

Serves 4

Ingredients

pepper

1 pound fish filets

2 tablespoons butter

paprika

sea salt

Tools

fry pan   tongs

Fish gives your body many important nutrients, including vitamin D, special fats and iodine. Iodine is a mineral that is missing from many foods, because the soil we grow our food in doesn't contain enough of it. But oceans are rich in iodine and foods that come from the ocean are also rich in this mineral.

1. Dry the fish with paper towels. Then sprinkle the fish all over with paprika, salt and pepper.

2. Put the butter in a fry pan. Put the pan on the stove over medium heat. Wait until the butter is bubbling, then add the fish to the pan.

3. Let the fish cook for about 5 minutes or until lightly browned, then flip it over using tongs. Let it cook on the other side for another 5 minutes.

4. Serve with tartar sauce (page 198), lemon butter sauce (page 59) or a squeeze of fresh lemon juice.

Shrimp Cocktail

Serves 4

Ingredients

12 large shrimp

½ cup ketchup (page 186) or ¾ cup lemon butter sauce (page 59)

filtered water

1 tablespoon sea salt

ice

Tools

cocktail glasses

bowl

slotted spoon

pot

Shrimp may be small, but they're loaded with nutrients, including vitamins D and B12, selenium, phosphorus, iron, protein and special fats. If you use shell-on shrimp, you can save the shells to make bone broth (page 108). Sardines, anchovies, clams, oysters and mussels are other foods from the ocean that are also very rich in vitamins and minerals.

1. If using frozen shrimp, let the shrimp thaw overnight in the refrigerator.

2. Put the salt and about 1 quart filtered water in a pot. Put the pot on the stove over high heat.

3. Wait until the water is boiling, then add the shrimp. Cook for about 5 minutes or until the shrimp turn bright pink and float to the top. Remove the shrimp with a slotted spoon and put them in a bowl of ice water.

4. If using shell-on shrimp, remove the legs and shells from the shrimp, but leave the tails on.

5. To serve, put a couple tablespoons of ketchup or lemon butter sauce in each cocktail glass. Then hang three shrimp on the rim of each glass.

Baked Chicken

Serves 6

Ingredients

1 whole chicken, cut into pieces

sea salt

pepper

Tools

glass baking dish

baster

Basting chicken in it's own juices or drippings keeps the meat moist while it bakes and makes the skin golden and crispy. Chicken should always be eaten with the skin. The skin contains healthy fat and many vitamins and minerals.

1. Place the chicken pieces skin-side up in a glass baking dish. Sprinkle with salt and pepper.

2. Bake in a 350-degree oven for 1½ hours or until golden brown. Baste the chicken about every 30 minutes with the drippings in the bottom of the dish.

Drippings

To make a sauce for the chicken, mix the drippings in a bowl with 1/4 cup honey and 1 tablespoon mustard. The drippings can also be used to make mashed potatoes (page 102). Or save them in a jar in the refrigerator for other uses. Once cold, they will become solid and separate into two layers. The top layer is fat. This can be used for cooking in place of butter or oil. The bottom layer is gelatin. This can be added to soups and sauces. Fat and gelatin help your body absorb nutrients from your food.

Roast Chicken

Serves 6

Ingredients

pepper

1 whole chicken
(about 4 pounds)

sea salt

Tools

wooden spoon

baster

casserole

Roasting chicken inside a casserole is a good way to cook a chicken for making bone broth (page 108). The meat stays very moist and is easy to remove from the bones.

1. Preheat the oven to 350 degrees.

2. Put the chicken in a casserole, breast-side down. Sprinkle salt and pepper on top. Then put the lid on the casserole.

3. Bake in the oven for 1 ½ hours.

4. Turn the chicken over using a wooden spoon (stick the spoon inside the cavity of the chicken, lift up and turn.) Then transfer the drippings in the bottom of the casserole to a bowl or jar using a baster. The drippings can be used to make a sauce or saved for other uses (see page 176).

5. Sprinkle more salt and pepper on top of the chicken. Return the chicken to the oven, without the lid on, and bake for 30 minutes or until the chicken is golden brown.

Chicken Curry

Serves 4

Ingredients

½ onion

about ½ chicken, cooked

1 apple

1 stalk celery

¼ cup crispy nuts (page 65)

chicken drippings

1 teaspoon curry powder

¼ teaspoon sea salt

1 tablespoon honey

Tools

spoon

knife

fry pan

cutting board

Turn those chicken leftovers into something exotic! Your belly will be dancing!

1. Peel the onion, then chop the chicken, onion, celery, apple and nuts into small pieces.

2. Put all the ingredients in a fry pan and mix together with a spoon.

3. Put the pan on the stove over medium heat. Cook, stirring occasionally, until the apple is soft.

More Recipes for Leftover Chicken
Chicken and Rice Soup (page 111)
Chicken Salad (page 193)
Bento Cobb Salad (page 197)

Meatballs

Serves 6

Meatballs are a favorite food around the world. You can serve them in soup like the Italians do or with potatoes and vegetables like the Dutch. You can bake them or fry them in a pan with some lard or coconut oil. You can make them really nourishing by including liver, a food rich in vitamins and minerals.

Ingredients

1 onion

1 pound ground beef or lamb

½ pound chicken liver (or ½ pound more ground beef or lamb)

1 cup bread crumbs

several sprigs parsley

1 teaspoon sea salt

butter or coconut oil

2 eggs

¼ teaspoon pepper

½ cup cream

Tools

spoon

knife

glass baking dish

mixing bowl

food processor

cutting board

1. Preheat the oven to 350 degrees.

2. To make the bread crumbs, put some leftover sourdough bread (such as crusts from making croutons) in a food processor until finely ground. Transfer the bread crumbs to a mixing bowl. Add the cream and mix together.

3. Peel the onion, then cut it into several large pieces. Remove the thick stems from the parsley. Put the onion and parsley in the food processor and pulse a few times until finely chopped. Transfer the onion and parsley to the mixing bowl.

4. Grind the liver in the food processor and add it to the mixing bowl.

5. Add the ground beef, eggs, salt and pepper, and mix everything together with a spoon or your hands.

6. Rub butter on the inside of a glass baking dish.

7. Using your hands, form the meat mixture into balls about the size of golf balls. Set the balls inside the baking dish.

8. Bake the meatballs in the oven for 30 minutes. Then turn the meatballs over and bake for another 30 minutes. Serve with ketchup or tomato sauce (page 186).

Sloppy Joe Casserole

Serves 6

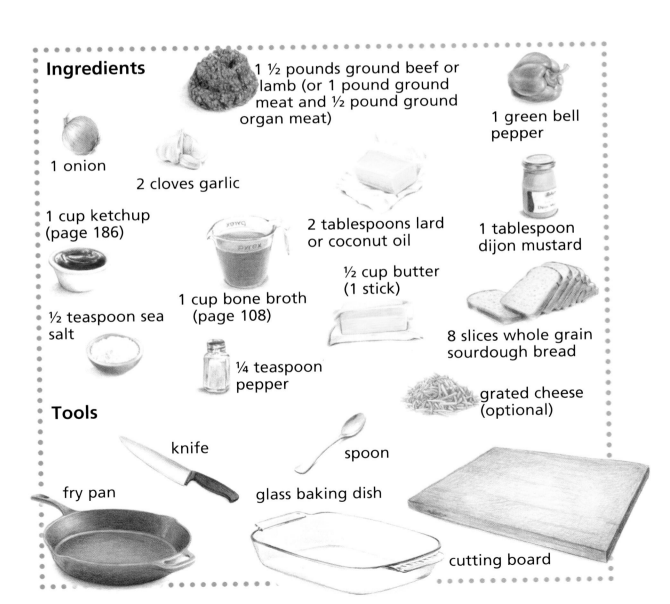

Ingredients

1 ½ pounds ground beef or lamb (or 1 pound ground meat and ½ pound ground organ meat)

1 green bell pepper

1 onion

2 cloves garlic

1 cup ketchup (page 186)

2 tablespoons lard or coconut oil

1 tablespoon dijon mustard

½ cup butter (1 stick)

1 cup bone broth (page 108)

8 slices whole grain sourdough bread

½ teaspoon sea salt

¼ teaspoon pepper

grated cheese (optional)

Tools

fry pan

knife

spoon

glass baking dish

cutting board

This casserole can be made ahead of time, refrigerated and baked just before serving.

1. Peel the onion and garlic. Remove the seeds and stem from the bell pepper. Then, chop the onion, bell pepper and garlic into small pieces.

2. Put the ground meat, chopped vegetables and lard in a fry pan. Put the pan on the stove over medium heat. Cook, stirring occasionally, until the meat is browned.

3. Add the broth and boil for 10 minutes or until the liquid is almost gone.

4. Add the ketchup, mustard, salt and pepper and mix together.

5. Put the butter in a glass baking dish. Put the baking dish in a warm oven for a few minutes until the butter melts.

6. Break the bread into pieces with your hands. Put the bread pieces in the baking dish and mix together with a spoon until all the bread is coated in butter.

7. Spoon the cooked meat on top of the bread.

8. Cover and refrigerate or bake immediately. Bake in a 350-degree oven for about 30 minutes or until the bread on the edges is crispy. Sprinkle cheese on top, if you like, and let melt before serving.

Beef Stew

Serves 6

Ingredients

6 carrots

2 pounds beef chuck, cut into 1-inch cubes

1 quart bone broth (page 108)

1 onion

1 cup apple juice

½ cup apple cider vinegar

12 baby red potatoes

2 tablespoons dijon mustard

1 teaspoon sea salt

½ teaspoon pepper

several sprigs thyme

vegetable brush

Tools

spoon

knife

cutting board

glass bowl

casserole

Tough cuts of meat, like beef chuck, can be made more tender by marinating in vinegar and cooking very slowly in broth. When you know how to make stew, you can call yourself an accomplished cook!

1. Put the meat in a glass bowl. Mix the apple juice and vinegar together and pour over the meat. Mix the meat with the liquid. Cover bowl and leave at room temperature for 3 - 4 hours or up to 24 hours in the refrigerator.

2. Remove the meat from the marinade and put it in the casserole. Discard the marinade.

3. Peel the onion and scrub the carrots; then cut the carrots and onion into 1-inch chunks. Add the carrots, onion, potatoes, mustard, salt, pepper and thyme to the casserole. Pour the broth over the top.

4. Cover the casserole with a lid and cook in a 250 degree oven for 6 - 12 hours.

Lamb Chops

Serves 4

Ingredients

pepper

8 lamb rib chops

sea salt

Tools

tongs

broiler pan

Lamb is still mostly raised on pastures and not in factory farms. If you only have access to meat from a supermarket, lamb is a good option. Try to find lamb chop with plenty of fat on the edges. The fat is the best part!

1. Preheat the broiler on your oven.

2. Pat the chops dry with paper towls. Then put the chops on a broiler pan and sprinkle with salt and pepper.

3. Place under the broiler for 5 minutes. Remove the pan from the oven and turn the chops over using tongs. Sprinkle with salt and pepper. Return the pan to the oven and broil for another 5 minutes.

Ketchup

Makes 1 ½ cups

Ingredients

1 7-ounce jar tomato paste

¼ cup apple cider vinegar

¼ cup maple syrup

½ teaspoon sea salt

½ teaspoon allspice

dash cayenne pepper

Tools

pint-sized jar

spoon

Store-bought ketchup has some mysterious ingredients in it. What exactly are "spices" and "natural flavorings?" They don't sound bad, but did you know that monosodium glutamate or MSG (a toxin that can hurt your brain) is allowed to be called a "natural flavor?" Most ketchups also contain high fructose corn syrup, a very unhealthy sweetener. And the squeezable plastic bottles they come in aren't good either. Since ketchup is acidic, the plastic can leech into the ketchup. It's best to make your own ketchup at home.

Put all the ingredients in a jar and mix together with a spoon.

Tomato Sauce
Add 1 cup bone broth (page 108) to turn this ketchup into a sauce.

My Healthy Lunch

My Healthy Lunch

You already know that eggs are an incredible food, that butter is better and that raw, whole milk is mighty good. But not everyone agrees that these foods are good for us. What kinds of foods do your friends eat? What kinds of foods are served at your school? Do you think the food at your school is healthy? If not, what would you change to make it better?

Many people believe saturated fat and cholesterol are bad for us. Because of this false belief, schools must limit the amount of saturated fat and cholesterol in the food they serve. This makes it very hard for schools to serve whole milk products, butter or eggs, because these foods are high in saturated fat and cholesterol. To stay within the limits, schools must serve low-fat or fat-free milk products and use vegetable oils or margarine instead of butter. Eggs are rarely served, because just one egg has more cholesterol in it than is allowed.

Instead of using zippered plastic bags that you throw away, pack your lunch in **reusable food containers** like a thermos or bento box. Reusable containers help save our environment and over time, save money too. A thermos keeps warm foods warm and cold foods cold. You can use it to bring leftover soup or stew. Heat the soup on the stove in the morning and then put it in the thermos. It will stay warm until lunchtime. Use a thermos to keep raw milk cold too.

Hopefully someday schools will serve truly healthy foods. Until then, it's best to bring your own lunch to school. If your friends or teachers ask why you do, you can show them your lunch and explain why it's healthier than the lunch served at school.

When packing your lunchbox you can pick and choose your favorite foods, because this is a meal just for you. It's a great way to learn how to build a balanced, complete meal. Try to include a variety of food from the four food groups below. This will help your body get all the nutrients it needs to be healthy and strong.

Don't forget to pack a healthy snack too. See Super Snacks (page 62) for recipes and ideas.

Animal Foods

Grains, Beans and Nuts

Fruits and Vegetables

Healthy Fat

Sandwiches

The sandwich is a pretty nifty invention. It's easy to take with you and it can include food from all the four food groups. Start with a healthy bread like whole grain sourdough bread or whole wheat pita bread. Spread plenty of butter, homemade mayonnaise (page 198), hummus (page 159) or mashed avocado on the bread to add healthy fat. Choose an animal food to put inside, like eggs, cheese or meat. Then make it colorful with vegetables. Fermented vegetables, like pickles and sauerkraut, are a good choice for meat sandwiches. The friendly bacteria in fermented vegetables help your body digest meat.

**Chicken or Fish Salad
(page 193)**

Salami and Mustard

Cheese and Cucumber

Roast Beef and Sauerkraut (page 130)

Egg Salad

Serves 4

Ingredients

1 ripe avocado (optional)

4 hard-boiled eggs (page 23)

1 or 2 pickled cucumbers (page 128)

¼ cup mayonnaise (page 198)

1 teaspoon Dijon mustard

dash pepper

¼-½ teaspoon sea salt

Tools

fork

knife

bowl

cutting board

1. Peel and slice the eggs.

2. If using avocado, peel and seed the avocado (see page 78 for instructions). The avocado will turn black after a few hours, so don't use avocado if you plan to save some of the salad for later.

3. Chop the pickled cucumbers into tiny pieces.

4. Put all the ingredients in a bowl and mix and mash together with a fork.

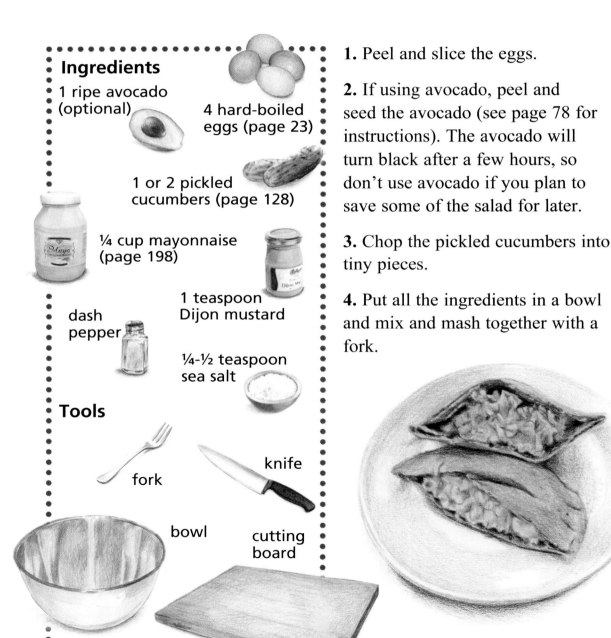

Chicken Salad

Serves 4

Ingredients

2 celery stalks

about ½ chicken, cooked (page 176)

¼ cup raisins

¼ cup crispy nuts (page 65)

¼ cup mayonnaise (page 198)

2 teaspoons Dijon mustard

Tools

knife

spoon

bowl

cutting board

1. Chop the chicken, celery and nuts into small pieces and put them in a bowl.

2. Add the raisins, mayonnaise and mustard.

3. Mix everything together with a spoon.

Fish Salad

Use leftover cooked fish, canned tuna or sardines instead of chicken.

Potato Salad

Serves 6

Made with eggs and plenty of healthy fats, this potato salad makes a nourishing side dish for a picnic or barbeque. Or pack it in your lunchbox with
a salami or roast beef sandwich.

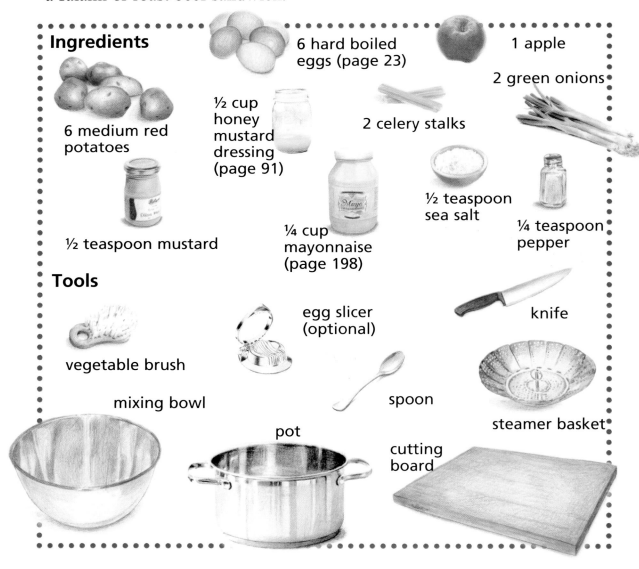

Ingredients

6 medium red potatoes

6 hard boiled eggs (page 23)

1 apple

½ cup honey mustard dressing (page 91)

2 celery stalks

2 green onions

½ teaspoon mustard

¼ cup mayonnaise (page 198)

½ teaspoon sea salt

¼ teaspoon pepper

Tools

vegetable brush

egg slicer (optional)

knife

mixing bowl

spoon

pot

cutting board

steamer basket

1. Scrub the potatoes clean with a vegetable brush (there is no need to peel them).

2. Fill a pot with about an inch of water. Set a steamer basket inside the pot. Then add the potatoes.

3. Put the pot on the stove over high heat until the water comes to a boil. Then cover the pot with a lid and cook over medium heat for about 30 minutes or until the potatoes are tender.

4. Allow the potatoes to cool. Then cut the potatoes into small pieces and put them in a mixing bowl.

5. Peel and slice the eggs using an egg slicer or a knife and add them to the mixing bowl.

6. Remove the ends from the green onions. Then chop the apple, celery and green onions into small pieces and add them to the mixing bowl.

7. Add the dressing, mayonnaise, mustard, salt and pepper. Mix everything together with a spoon.

8. Cover the bowl with a plate or lid and chill in the refrigerator before serving.

Traditional Bento

Serves 1

Ingredients

½ cup cooked brown rice (page 154)

cooked fish, chicken or meat

fresh, fermented or cooked vegetables

dressing, dip or sauce made with healthy fat

Tools

bento box

knife

cutting board

1. Fill one of the compartments of the bento box with rice.

2. Put the fish, chicken or meat in another compartment.

3. Put the vegetables in another compartment.

4. Drizzle the dressing or sauce on top or keep it in a separate compartment for dipping.

In Japan, it's common to eat bento for lunch. A traditional bento includes rice, fish or meat and fermented or cooked vegetables. The food is packed inside a reusable food container, called a bento box, which has several smaller compartments inside. A bento box with four compartments can help you remember to include food from each of the four food groups. If you have time, you can arrange the food in a creative way to make it look like animals or flowers, as Japanese mothers often do when making bento for their children.

Cobb Salad Bento

Serves 1

Ingredients

lettuce

tomato

cooked chicken (page 176)

cheese

hard boiled egg (page 23)

avocado

bacon

honey mustard dressing (page 91)

Tools

knife

mini cookie cutters (optional)

bento box

cutting board

1. Cut the lettuce into shreds and put a bit of lettuce in each compartment.

2. Cut the other ingredients into different shapes, using a knife or mini cookie cutters, and arrange them on top of the lettuce to make animals, flowers, etc.

3. Drizzle the honey mustard dressing on top.

Mayonnaise

Makes 1 ½ cups

Ingredients

1 cup
sour cream

2 egg yolks

¼ cup
extra-virgin
olive oil

¼ cup raw
apple cider
vinegar

1 tablespoon
Dijon mustard

½ teaspoon
sea salt

1 tablespoon
raw honey

Tools

pint-sized
glass jar

Most mayonnaise is made with unhealthy vegetable oils like canola and soy. Here's an easy mayonnaise you can make at home using healthy fats.

Put all the ingredients in a glass jar. Close the jar tightly with a lid and shake to mix together.

Tartar Sauce

Add 1 or 2 chopped pickled cucumbers (page 128) to turn this mayonnaise into a delicious tartar sauce for fish.

What's for Dessert?

What's for Dessert?

What is your favorite dessert? Do you know what ingredients are in it? Most desserts are very sweet and made with ingredients like refined sugar and flour, high fructose corn syrup and vegetable oil. These are empty ingredients. They give your body energy, but very few vitamins, minerals or other nutrients that you need to be healthy and strong. In fact, desserts with lots of sugar in them can actually take nutrients away from your body and make you tired soon after. As you may remember from the Super Snacks chapter (page 63), your body needs minerals to digest sugar. What will your body do if it can't get these minerals

from your food? It will take them out of your teeth and bones! Eating empty, sugary foods can cause tooth decay and easily broken bones. It can also lead to infections, weight gain, diabetes and many other health problems.

If we want to be healthy, then, can we still eat dessert? Desserts don't have to be empty, sugary foods. Butter, cream, eggs, fresh fruit, coconut, soaked whole grains and small amounts of natural sweeteners can be used to make delicious desserts that are full of vitamins and minerals and low in sugar. The recipes in this chapter will show you how.

Remember, though, even a healthy dessert should only be enjoyed after eating a nourishing meal. Eating dessert

Blood Sugar Roller Coaster
Did you know that your blood has sugar in it? The sugar in your blood gives your body energy to move and gives your brain energy to think. When your blood has the right amount of sugar in it, you feel good and energetic. When your blood doesn't have enough sugar in it, you feel tired and hungry.

Your blood sugar goes up and down depending on the food you eat. When you eat foods that digest quickly, like a dessert with lots of sugar or flour in it, your blood sugar goes up very quickly. Your body doesn't need all this sugar at once, so it removes the extra sugar and stores it as fat on your body. Sometimes, if your blood sugar goes up too fast, your body panics and removes too much sugar. Then you feel very tired. It's like going up and down on a roller coaster. First you have too much energy, then you have none. This is very bad for your body and may lead to a disease called diabetes. To avoid the blood sugar roller coaster, eat foods that have fat or protein in them, like desserts made with butter, cream and eggs instead of desserts made with mostly sugar and flour. Eating a nourishing meal before eating your dessert will also help.

before dinner, especially a rich dessert made with lots of cream or butter, might make you too full to finish your dinner. The word dessert comes from an old French word, *desservir*, meaning "to clear the table." A good routine to follow is to serve dessert only after everyone has finished eating and helped to clear the table. Another good habit is to enjoy your dessert with a glass of raw milk. Cheers!

Guide to Natural Sweeteners

Natural sweeteners are better than refined sweeteners, because they contain minerals and other nutrients. But be careful not to add too much. Most sweeteners, even natural ones, contain about 4 grams of sugar per teaspoon. A good rule to follow is add no more than 8 grams (2 teaspoons) of sugar per serving.

Maple Syrup and Maple Sugar

Maple syrup and maple sugar are made from the sap of maple trees. The sap is full of minerals, brought up from the ground by the tree's deep roots. Organic maple syrup is best because it's made without any chemicals. Use only real maple syrup. Avoid imitations, like "maple flavored" pancake, waffle or table syrup, which are made with high fructose corn syrup and artificial flavors.

Honey

Did you know that honey is an animal food, like milk? That's because it's made by bees. And just like milk, honey is best when it's raw. It contains enzymes and other nutrients that are destroyed by heat. Use honey in recipes that will not be cooked or add it to the food after it's cooked. The enzymes in honey help your body digest grains. Honey also contains trace amounts of pollen that can help prevent seasonal allergies, especially if the honey comes from bees near where you live.

Dehydrated Cane Sugar Juice

This sweetener is simply cane sugar juice that has been dried and broken into crystals. It is usually sold under the names Rapadura or Sucanat. It is not the same as evaporated cane sugar juice, turbinado, raw sugar or brown sugar. These are all refined sweeteners that have had their natural minerals removed.

Molasses

Molasses is what's leftover when refined sugar is made. It contains many minerals, including iron and calcium. It has a strong flavor, so it's best used in combination with another natural sweetener like maple syrup. Organic, unsulfured molasses is best.

Sugar substitutes like Splenda (sucralose) and Nutra-Sweet (aspartame) may seem like healthy options, because they don't contain any sugar or calories, but do you know how they work? Sugar substitutes are more like drugs than food, they trick your brain into thinking it's tasting sugar when it's not. And just like drugs, they can hurt your body, including your brain, liver and kidneys.

Ice Cream

Makes 1 quart

Ingredients

1 cup raw milk (or for a richer ice cream, 1 cup more cream)

2 cups cream

4 egg yolks

¼ – ½ cup maple syrup or honey

1 tablespoon vanilla extract

Tools

whisk

4 cup glass measuring cup

ice cream maker or popsicle molds

Store-bought ice cream usually has a lot of sugar in it and fillers to make it seem creamy, even though very little cream is actually used. However, ice cream made at home with small amounts of natural sweeteners and plenty of cream from grassfed animals is actually a healthy treat. Raw cream is best, but pasteurized is okay too, just avoid ultra-pasteurized. It's important to use eggs from healthy chickens, too, especially since this recipe uses them raw.

1. Put the ingredients in a glass measuring cup and mix together with a whisk.

2. Pour into an ice cream maker and follow the manufacturer's instructions. Or to make ice cream pops, pour into popsicle molds and freeze. Store ice cream in a plastic container in the freezer.

Fruit Ice Cream

Instead of milk, add 1 cup chopped or mashed fruit, such as strawberries, bananas, peaches, mangos or persimmons.

Carob Ice Cream

Add ¼ cup carob powder and 1 teaspoon chocolate extract. Use a blender to make the mixture smooth.

Frozen Yogurt

Use 1 cup plain yogurt or kefir (page 41) instead of milk.

Whipped Cream

Makes 1 cup

Whipped cream from a can may be quick and easy, but have you read what's in it? Are you sure you want to top your dessert with high fructose corn syrup, artificial flavors and mono- and diglycerides? Real whipped cream is made with just three simple ingredients: cream, a natural sweetener and vanilla. If you have a food processor, it takes less than a minute to make!

Put the cream and syrup in a bowl and beat with a whisk until thick. Or put the ingredients in a food processor and pulse until thick.

Peaches 'n' Cream
Cut up some fresh peaches, strawberries or other fruit and serve with a bowl of whipped cream for dipping.

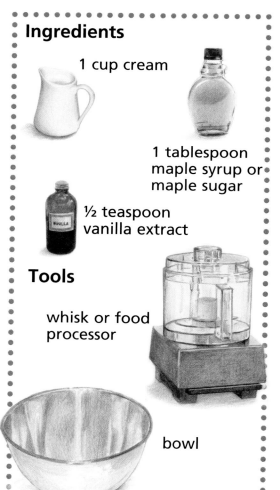

Ingredients

1 cup cream

1 tablespoon maple syrup or maple sugar

½ teaspoon vanilla extract

Tools

whisk or food processor

bowl

Coconut Pops

Makes 6
popsicles

Ingredients

1 can organic
whole coconut milk

¾ cup coconut
water

¼ cup
maple syrup

Tools

4-cup glass
measuring cup

spoon

popsicle molds

These popsicles are especially good to eat when you have a cold or sore throat. Coconuts contain a special fat that helps your body fight bad bacteria.

Put the ingredients in a glass measuring cup or a bowl with a pour spout. Mix together with a spoon. Pour into popsicle molds and freeze for at least 4 hours.

Water Kefir Pops

Pour Grape Cooler (page 138) or Coconut Cocktail (page 140) into popsicle molds and freeze.

Coconut Cookies

Makes 1 dozen

Ingredients

2 egg whites

1 teaspoon vanilla extract

1 cup unsweetened shredded coconut

3 tablespoons maple syrup

Tools

spoon

jar

fork

bowl

parchment paper

cookie sheet

These cookies are a great way to use up leftover egg whites from other recipes.

1. Preheat the oven to 300 degrees.

2. Put the egg whites, syrup and vanilla in a jar. Close the jar tightly with a lid. Shake the jar until the mixture is foamy.

3. Pour the mixture into a bowl. Add the shredded coconut and mix together with a spoon.

4. Line a cookie sheet with parchment paper.

5. Drop spoonfuls of the coconut mixture onto the cookie sheet. Then poke lots of holes into the cookies using a fork.

6. Bake for 25 minutes or until golden brown on the edges.

Butter Cookies

Makes 1 dozen

Ingredients

¼ cup butter (½ stick)

¾ cup spelt or whole wheat pastry flour

2 tablespoons kefir (page 41), whey (page 44), buttermilk (page 56) or yogurt

¼ cup dehydrated sugar cane juice

½ teaspoon vanilla extract

pinch sea salt

Tools

mixing bowl

grain mill (optional)

spoon

cookie sheet

parchment paper

Spelt or whole wheat pastry flour (flour made from soft white wheat berries) works best for this recipe because it has a softer texture than other whole grain flours.

1. Put the butter in a mixing bowl. Put the bowl in a warm oven until the butter is soft.

2. If using a grain mill to make fresh flour, grind ½ cup spelt or soft white wheat berries to make ¾ cup flour.

3. Add the flour and cultured milk to the melted butter. Mix together with a spoon. Cover the bowl with a towel or plate and leave in a warm place for 8 - 24 hours.

4. Add the dehydrated cane sugar juice, vanilla and salt to the soaked dough and mix together.

5. Line a cookie sheet with parchment paper.

6. Roll the dough into small balls and place on the cookie sheet. Flatten the balls with the back of a spoon.

7. Bake in a 350-degree oven for about 15 minutes or until the edges of the cookies are golden.

Nut Butter Cookies
Add ½ cup crispy nut butter (page 68).

Spice Cookies
Add 2 tablespoons unsulphured molasses, ½ teaspoon cinnamon, ¼ teaspoon nutmeg, ¼ teaspoon ginger and a pinch of cloves.

Frosting
Put 1/2 cup butter (softened at room temperature, but not melted), 2 tablespoons raw honey or maple syrup and 1 teaspoon vanilla extract in a bowl. Beat together with a whisk for several minutes. Wait until the cookies have cooled before frosting. Shredded coconut makes great sprinkles!

Oatmeal Raisin Cookies

Makes 1 dozen

Ingredients

¼ cup butter (½ stick)

1 cup rolled oats

¼ cup raisins

½ cup kefir (page 41), whey (page 44), buttermilk (page 56) or yogurt

3 tablespoons dehydrated sugar cane juice

1 egg

½ teaspoon baking soda

½ teaspoon vanilla

Tools

spoon

mixing bowl

parchment paper

cookie sheet

These chewy cookies are made only with oatmeal, no other grain or flour is used. They can be made gluten-free by using gluten-free oats.

1. Put the butter in a mixing bowl. Put the bowl in a warm oven until the butter is soft.

2. Add the oats, cultured milk and raisins to the melted butter. Mix together with a spoon. Cover the bowl with a towel or plate and leave in a warm place for 8 - 24 hours.

3. Add the eggs, dehydrated sugar cane juice, vanilla and baking soda and mix together.

4. Line a cookie sheet with parchment paper.

5. Drop spoonfuls of the dough on the cookie sheet. Leave space around the cookies, as they will spread when baking.

6. Bake in a 300-degree oven for about 30 minutes or until the cookies are golden.

Sourdough Cookies
Add 2 tablespoons sourdough starter when soaking the oats. Fresh milk or water can be used instead of cultured milk.

Carob Brownies

Makes 1 dozen

Ingredients

½ cup coconut oil

½ cup butter (1 stick)

¾ cup carob powder

½ cup dehydrated sugar cane juice

1 teaspoon vanilla extract

4 eggs

pinch sea salt

1 teaspoon chocolate extract

Tools

whisk

8-inch square baking pan

mixing bowl

parchment paper

mesh strainer

Shhh, don't tell anyone, but these brownies don't have any chocolate in them. They're made with a rich flourless base of butter, coconut oil and eggs and flavored with carob and chocolate extract. You'll definitely need a glass of milk with these!

1. Put the butter and coconut oil in a mixing bowl. Put the bowl in a warm oven until the butter and oil completely melt.

2. Place a mesh strainer over the bowl. Put the carob powder in the strainer and stir it with a whisk until all the powder falls into the bowl below. This will remove any clumps from the powder.

3. Add the dehydrated sugar cane juice, vanilla, chocolate extract and salt. Mix together with a whisk.

4. Add the eggs and mix together.

5. Line a baking pan with parchment paper. Then pour the batter into the baking pan.

6. Bake in a 350-degree oven for about 30 minutes.

7. Let cool, then cover and refrigerate until firm. Cut into squares to serve.

Applesauce

Makes 1 quart

Ingredients

6 tart apples

1 cup apple juice

½ teaspoon cinnamon

Tools

knife

spoon

pot

blender or food processor

cutting board

Applesauce is one dessert you can eat with your dinner. It makes a delicious side dish with meat and potatoes. Or enjoy it after dinner with whipped cream (page 206).

1. Cut the apples into chunks and put them in a pot.

2. Add the apple juice and cinnamon.

3. Put the pot on the stove over high heat until the juice comes to a boil. Then cover the pot with a lid and cook over low heat until the apples are soft.

4. Puree the cooked apples and juice in a blender or food processor. Or blend right in the pot using a handheld blender.

Parfait

Serves 6

Ingredients

1 tablespoon unflavored, unsweetened gelatin

1 ½ cups fruit juice

2 cups chopped fruit

1 ½ cups whipped cream (page 206)

Tools

knife

sauce pan

6 juice glasses

spoon

cutting board

To make a parfait,
Fill a glass with fruit half-way.
Add gelatin and cream,
And you have dessert
Fit for a king or queen!

Berries, bananas, peaches and grapes are all good fruits to use for making gelatin parfaits. If you want to use tropical fruits (like pineapple, mango, papaya, guava or kiwi) you'll need to cook them first. Otherwise, enzymes in these fruits can prevent the gelatin from gelling.

1. Put the juice and gelatin in a sauce pan with a pour spout.

2. Put the pan on the stove over medium heat, stirring often, until the juice comes to a simmer, but be careful not to let the juice boil.

3. Allow the dissolved gelatin to cool for about 10 minutes.

Know Your Ingredients
Can you guess what product this is? The ingredients are sugar, gelatin, adipic acid, artificial flavor, disodium phosphate, sodium citrate, fumaric acid, red 40.

It's JELL-O Brand Strawberry Flavored Gelatin. It's sweetened with white sugar (nearly 20 grams per serving), flavored with artificial chemicals (not real strawberries) and it gets its bright red color from artificial food dye. It also contains several other chemical additives that are difficult to pronounce. Foods containing artificial ingredients like these have been shown to cause behavioral problems in children and should be avoided.

4. Meanwhile, chop the fruit into small chunks.

5. Fill each glass half-way with the chopped fruit. Then pour the dissolved gelatin over the fruit. Leave the top half of the glass empty.

6. Chill in the refrigerator for about 4 hours or until the gelatin is firm.

7. Just before serving, fill the top of each glass with whipped cream (page 206).

Apple Cobbler

Serves 6

Ingredients

4 tart apples

1 dozen butter or nut butter cookies (page 210)

¼ cup butter (½ stick)

¼ teaspoon cinnamon

2 tablespoons dehydrated cane sugar juice

Tools

9 inch pie pan or baking dish

knife

cutting board

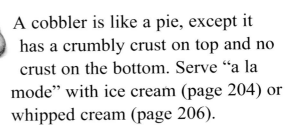

A cobbler is like a pie, except it has a crumbly crust on top and no crust on the bottom. Serve "a la mode" with ice cream (page 204) or whipped cream (page 206).

1. Pre-heat the oven to 350 degrees.

2. Rub butter on the inside of a pie or baking dish.

3. Cut the apples into thin slices and put them in the baking dish.

4. Cut the butter into thin slices and layer it on top of the apples.

5. Sprinkle the dehydrated cane sugar juice and cinnamon on top.

6. Bake for about 45 minutes or until the apples are soft.

7. Crumble the cookies on top and bake for another 5 - 10 minutes just before serving.

Peach Cobbler
Use peaches instead of apples.

Egg Custard

Serves 6

Ingredients

6 egg yolks

2 cups cream

¼ cup maple syrup

1 teaspoon vanilla extract

nutmeg or cinnamon

Tools

6 ramekins (6-ounce)

mixing bowl

wire whisk

baking pan

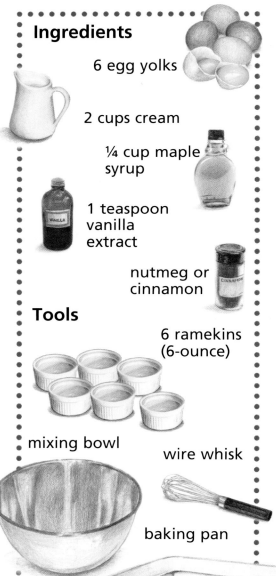

This dreamy dessert is baked in the oven in special dishes called ramekins. The ramekins are placed in a pan of water to keep the custard moist while it bakes.

1. Preheat the oven to 275 degrees.

2. Mix the eggs, cream, maple syrup and vanilla in a mixing bowl with a wire whisk.

3. Pour an equal amount into each ramekin.

4. Place the ramekins in a baking pan and fill the pan with hot water until the water is about ½ inch deep.

5. Bake for 1 hour. Have an adult transfer the pan to and from the oven.

6. Sprinkle with nutmeg or cinnamon and drizzle more maple syrup on top. Chill in the refrigerator before serving.

Bread Pudding

Serves 6

Ingredients

3 cups whole grain sourdough bread

1 cup cream

3 eggs

2 teaspoons vanilla extract

¼ cup maple syrup

1 teaspoon cinnamon

Tools

6 ramekins (6-ounce)

spoon

wire whisk

mixing bowl

baking pan

This recipe can be prepared in advance, refrigerated and then baked just before serving. Bread pudding is best when the bread is allowed to soak for awhile.

1. Mix the eggs, cream, syrup, vanilla and cinnamon in a bowl with a whisk.

2. Tear the bread into bite-size chunks until you have about 3 cups. Add the bread to the bowl and mix together.

3. Cover the bowl with a towel or plate and let sit for 30 minutes or longer in the refrigerator.

4. Spoon an equal amount of the pudding into each ramekin.

5. Place the ramekins in a baking pan and fill the pan with hot water until the water is about ½ inch deep.

6. Bake in a 350-degree oven for about 30 minutes or until the tops are golden. Have an adult transfer the pan to and from the oven. Serve warm or chilled.

Sources

The healthiest foods are often the most difficult to find, like raw milk and whole grain sourdough bread. Sources for these foods can be found in the Weston A. Price Foundation Shopping Guide (available from westona-price.org) or the WAPF Find Real Food App (available on the iPhone from the App Store). Your local WAPF chapter may also know of sources specific to your area.

Kefir Grains

Contact your local WAPF chapter for sources in your area. Dehydrated kefir grains are also available for purchase from Cultures for Health (culturesforhealth.com).

Grain Mills

The WonderMill (thewondermill.com)
The Family Grain Mill
(grainmill.com)

Dehydrators

Excalibur (excaliburdehydrator.com)

Kraut Pounder

The WAPF Eugene Chapter makes these and sells them as a fundraiser for their chapter (krautpounder.com)

Recipe Index

clarified butter 58
cobbler, apple 219
cobbler, peach 219
cobb salad bento 197
coconut chips 73
coconut cocktail 140
coconut cookies 208
coconut pops 207
coconut rice 154
coconut soup 110
cookies, butter 210
cookies, coconut 208
cookies, nut butter 211
cookies, oatmeal raisin 212
cookies, sourdough 213
cookies, spice 211
corn on the cob, fresh 100
cottage cheese 45
crackers, rice 76
crackers, seaweed 77
cream cheese 43
cream cheese dip 71
cream cheese dressing 92
cream, whipped 206
crispy nut butter 68
crispy nuts 65
croutons 121
cucumbers, pickled 128
custard, egg 220

D
deviled eggs 24
dip, bean 159
dip, cream cheese 71
dressing, avocado 93
dressing, honey mustard 91
dressing, cream cheese 92

E
egg custard 220
egg-dipped French toast 27
egg drop soup 120
egg eyes 26
eggnog 34
egg salad 192
eggs, boiled 23
eggs, deviled 24
eggs, fried 26
eggs, Mexican scrambled 21
eggs, ruby 25
eggs, scrambled 19
egg yolk smoothie 33

F
fish, pan-fried 174
fish salad 193
fish, teriyaki 172
French toast 27
fried eggs 26
frosting 211
frozen yogurt 205
fruit and cheese kabobs 83
fruit ice cream 205
fruit rolls 80
fruit snacks 79

G
ginger ale 139
grape cooler 138
Greek omelet 29
guacamole 78

H
honey butter spread 57
honey mustard dressing 91
hummus 159

About the Authors

Catherine Lacey Photography

SUZANNE GROSS lives in Los Angeles with her husband, Ziv, and their three children, Ariella, Natalie and Ethan. For as long as she can remember, she has loved books and music and has written numerous short stories, poems and songs. Cooking became one of her passions when she realized it was a necessary skill to have in order to keep her family healthy. She holds a bachelor's degree in Library and Information Science and at one time was planning to become a school librarian. She still thinks being a librarian or a teacher would be one of the best jobs in the world, second only to being a mom of course. This is her first book.

SALLY FALLON MORELL is the author of the best-selling cookbook *Nourishing Traditions* (with Mary G. Enig, PhD) and has become the number one voice for a return to nutrient-dense foods in the industrial age.

She also co-authored *The Fourfold Path to Healing* (with Thomas S. Cowan, MD and Jaimen McMillan); *Eat Fat Lose Fat* (with Mary G. Enig, PhD); *The Nourishing Traditions Book of Baby & Child Care* (with Thomas S. Cowan, MD) and *Nourishing Broth* (with Kaayla T. Daniel, PhD, CCN). She hopes that these books will be of interest and help to all the children who learn to cook using *The Nourishing Traditions Cookbook for Children*. She also looks forward to the day when these children become members of the Weston A. Price Foundation, which she founded in 1999.

About the Illustrators

ANGELA SETTE EISENBART was educated in her homeland of Italy in marketing, graphic design and fine arts. She worked in studios in Milan, Italy and New York City before settling down in the Washington DC area working as graphic designer and illustrator for a four hundred-page monthly magazine. For the last fifteen years she has dedicated herself to teaching arts & crafts, graphic design and technical drawing at a small private school in Maryland, while constantly working to perfect her painting and drawing skills in different media. As a freelance artist she continues to serve a variety of clients with projects large and small.

KIM WATERS distinctive paintings draw freely from Medieval and Renaissance illuminations, Indian miniature painting, Celtic folklore, and Victorian book design and fairy tales. Her unique combination of Western alchemical symbols, and intricate borders introduces the viewer to a rich and intriguing fantasy world. Kim's illustrated publications include, *Illuminations from the Bhagavad-Gita*, now part of the permanent collection of The Museum of Sacred Art in Europe, *The Butter Thief, Enchanted Tales*, and numerous private commissions. Most notable are her cover designs for the *Nourishing Traditions* books of Sally Fallon Morell.

Acknowledgements

The Nourishing Traditions Cookbook for Children is published with sincere gratitude to my friend, Jenilyn, who introduced me to Ramiel Nagel's fascinating book *Cure Tooth Decay*, which ultimately led me to *Nourishing Traditions* and forever changed my concept of healthy food. Special thanks to Wardeh Harmon and Jami Delgado at the Gnowfglins Traditional Cooking School, who make the seemingly overwhelming task of preparing traditional foods easier and attainable, even with children. Thanks to my husband, Ziv, who lovingly eats everything I cook, even the failed attempts. And to my three very honest children, Ariella, Natalie and Ethan, for testing recipes with me. And to my mom, for her input and for keeping the children occupied so I could write. And of course, immense thanks to Sally Fallon Morell, who paved the way and graciously allowed me the opportunity to adapt her book into a children's version, and for her mindful edits and direction. And where would any of us be if it weren't for Dr. Weston A. Price, whose discoveries led to many wise conclusions, notably, "life in all its fullness is this Mother Nature obeyed" and whose last request, "you teach, you teach, you teach," we all strive to fulfill.

Suzanne Gross

This book combines the considerable talents of Suzanne Gross, Angela Eisenbart and Kim Waters. It has been especially gratifying to work as a team with Suzanne and Angela. Thank you Suzanne for your vision and skill in putting this book together, and to Angela for your immense artistic talent. Thanks also to the many supporters of *Nourishing Traditions*, whose encouragement and appreciation have kept me on track in this exhilarating journey over the years. And much gratitude to my husband Geoffrey Morell for his unfailing support.

Sally Fallon Morell

I would like to acknowledge my family, friends and well wishers for their encourage-ment and favors large and small during my work on this book. I extend my heartfelt thanks to all of you.

Angela Eisenbart

Notes

Notes